ALSO BY

# Carl Becker

Political Parties in the Province of New York from
1766–75 (1908)

Beginnings of the American People (1915)

Eve of the Revolution (1918)

Our Great Experiment in Democracy (1924)

The Declaration of Independence — A Study in the
History of Political Ideas (1922, 1942)

The Spirit of '76 (*with G. M. Clark and W. E. Dodd*)
(1926)

Modern History (1931)

The Heavenly City of the Eighteenth Century Philosophers (1932)

Every Man His Own Historian (1935)

Story of Civilization (*with Frederic Duncalf*) (1938)

Modern Democracy (1941)

New Liberties for Old (1941)

Cornell University: Founders and the Founding (1943)

How New Will the Better World Be? (1944)

Freedom and Responsibility in the American Way of
Life (1945)

# *Progress and Power*

# PROGRESS

## *AND*

# POWER

By CARL BECKER

*Introduction by LEO GERSHOY*

1949  *ALFRED A. KNOPF*  New York

THIS IS A BORZOI BOOK,
PUBLISHED BY ALFRED A. KNOPF, INC.

FIRST BORZOI EDITION

*Originally published in 1936 by the Stanford University Press. This edition reset and reprinted from new plates, together with an introduction.*

TO

MAUDE HEPWORTH RANNEY

*who possesses and has needed*

*forbearance and understanding*

NEITHER *the naked hand nor the understanding left to itself can effect much. It is by instruments and helps that the work is done. . . . Human knowledge and human power meet in one.*

FRANCIS BACON

# Introduction

By LEO GERSHOY

A CRISIS of values confronted liberals in the mid-thirties. Of this Carl Becker was not unaware, when he wrote *Progress and Power*, for in that drear decade it would have been difficult for a political literate, who was not wholly irresponsible, to ignore the desperate challenge of totalitarianism to liberal democracy. So in answering the sardonic inquiry, which he had phrased in his own unmistakable way, what if anything could be said for the human race, Becker was rallying to the defense of the doctrine of progress against the attack of rival credos.

What indeed was one to say, as the solid rationalist foundations laid in the eighteenth century and the massive edifice of democracy raised by the nineteenth-century liberals crumbled before one's eyes? What was the outlook in the years immediately ahead for the complex of forms, institutions, attitudes, and practices which made up the culture pattern of the Atlantic Community?

To determine where man was headed, one had first to discover where he had started from and when. Hence one consulted the record — at least if one was a historian — for how other than by scrutinizing the past could one get his outlook for the future? Still, the perspective of time alone did not suffice to place man in the necessary setting. A perspective of distance was also required, a distance sufficiently remote so that the reporter would not become emotionally involved in the activities he noted, yet not so far away that he could not report with accuracy the significant deeds that had taken place.

In the interests of historical objectivity Becker conjured up an impartial observer whom he stationed at a happy point of vantage along the cool Olympian Heights. From there he looked down upon the human scene and, divesting himself of the ideas which fashioned man's judgment and the passions which marred it, he simply noted memorable deeds and recorded the difference in character and extent between man's activities at the beginning of the long adventure and at the end. With a mock concern for scientific reckoning, Becker also made those calculations in terms of a time scale of 506,000 years, the impressionistic 500,000 allotted to precivilization rigorously checked by the exact 6,000 that he assigned to the civilized era. The recorded difference in man's activities would be the measure of human progress.

In what seemed a moment of flippancy Becker read the report of the observer as indicating that at the end of 506,000 years man had learned to put his remote ape-like ancestors into cages, while he observed their antics from the outside. This conclusion was possibly not couched in his most philosophical vein, but it did contain the kernel of his philosophical concern with the use and abuse of power. Power, he noted, was one great measure of difference. By itself power was not baleful. Destructive it had often been and threatened to be again; and of its concentration in reckless hands there was frequently little question. Yet there was no escaping it. Without power there could have been no progress; and whether progress or no in the future, power would remain.

Power, however, could not be separated from reason. From the very start, Becker pointed out, as man had sought new sources of power, he had constantly re-enforced his original equipment with new implements of power devised by his reason. Reason was always related to power, limited by it and contingent on it. At all times, so the record showed, the expansion of intelligence was as much conditioned by the multiplication of the implements of power as the multiplication of the implements of power was conditioned by the expansion of intelligence. But a breakdown of this interpendence impended at the present moment, a present that had begun 300 years or so ago. The intellectual capacity of man to modify his outlook, even his way of life, in itself greatly expanded and accelerated, was not only paralleled but exceeded by his potential to tap and utilize new sources of power. Hence the immediate problem before humanity was not with Lord Acton to rue what power had done to man or perhaps he with it, but to devise ways for controlling it or at least coming to terms with it on a reasonable basis for the future. Man would have to call on the resources of his reason to redress the balance of the old relationship.

The odds were not insuperable, for as one reviewed the four periods into which Becker had divided the time scale, a certain recurrent rhythm in the affairs of men became apparent. Periods of stability followed those of quickened change; and there were moments, 10,000 years or 100,000, when the primacy of power yielded to the less disruptive initiative of reason. Now, at the end of 506,000 years, as man faced the "x" years of an unexpired fourth period, the signs pointed to a new round of stabilization. Man's thinking could after a fashion adjust itself to new power relations. The important thing for the present was that he travel light on the new power train and, while taking some heed that it keep on the tracks, adapt himself to its direction and tempo. In time, sobered by economic

## Introduction

dislocation and strife and according to the rhythm established by the new technological civilization, man would learn to apply to his world of social relations the same matter-of-fact knowledge that had enabled his ancestors to reduce to orderliness and predictability the world of material nature. Humanity would be saved; all that would be lost was the idea of progress.

To readers familiar with the main contours of Becker's thinking this disillusioned diagram of the rise and fall of the doctrine of progress offered little that was new. It was neither an innocent intellectual journey nor an emergency conclusion hastily improvised to cope with an exigent need. It was of a piece with earlier views. Mankind, said Becker, having negotiated the first half million years, would last out the academic year. With the world so heavily laden, it could bear the additional burden of a book. The way of life of western man would not survive exactly as it had been delineated in the sacred writings of liberalism, but survive it would as it had arisen, by harmonizing man's reason with his power. If the terms were far more severe than they had been before, they were not altogether exorbitant; and in any case there would always be a future.

That conclusion had slowly been forming in Becker's mind. Though he said that a passage in Keynes'

## Introduction

*Essays in Persuasion* directly suggested the lectures that made up *Progress and Power,* it seemed reasonable to look for intimations of those views in his own essays. For example, his brilliant "Mr. Wells and the New History," written in 1921, clearly reveals that the seeds of many of his mature ideas had already been planted.

In that searching study Becker first presented in capsule form his ideas on the subjective character of thinking and the purposive and selective activity that entered into the writing of history. What, he inquired, was the purpose that inspired Wells to examine the vicissitudes of mankind and to write about its triumphs? Did he hold himself, as the manuals enjoined historians to do, dispassionately aloof, or was he emotionally implicated in the course and the outcome of the process under consideration? Obviously, answered Becker, Wells was not objective. He was on the contrary most idealistically biased and involved up to the hilt in a particular Wellsian way in the purposes, desires, and aspirations of the mankind he loved with such irritable and irritating indulgence. He was reexamining its past with an eye to future prospects, in the heart-warming thought of making effective use of humanity's heritage. So keenly and ardently did he wish to enlist the experience of mankind in the serv-

ice of its destiny that he felt within his scholarly
rights in roundly berating history when some of its
characters, like that Corsican fellow Napoleon, behaved less well than they should have — should have
behaved, that is, according to Wells' own precious
conviction that historical experience most clearly il-
lustrated the triumphant progress of man.

Mr. Wells, it was obvious, was as amiably confident
about the future as he was vigorously certain about
the past, particularly the institutions and the practices
that he disliked. Alas, it was not the study of history
that imposed upon his consciousness the glorious vision of a world state directed by disciplined intelligence and consecrated to the prosperity and happiness
of its members. Nor was impartial history speaking
through an experienced, observant, and scientifically-
minded British reporter. An indomitable cosmopoli-
tan and friend of man was averting his eyes with relief
from a drab present of war and nationalist hatreds to
seek from the pattern he had woven of the past such
balm of the spirit as he could find for the future. Perhaps, as he put it, the light of a new dawn was break-
ing slowly, "shining through the shutters of a dis-
ordered room." Perhaps, echoed Becker, but "those
shutters — how with ineffectual fingers we still fum-
ble at the unyielding clasps."

## Introduction

By implying delicately that the doctrine of progress might no longer be tenable, Becker was reaching out for a thought which, in time, with the aid of a catastrophic depression and some unprogressive revolutions, matured in the pages of *Progress and Power*. In the essay on Wells the germ of another less depressing thought was also present: the interdependence of man's thinking and his power relations. Of intelligence as the indispensable factor in progress Wells had written much in his *Outline*, too much probably for Becker. Of power, on the other hand, good liberal that he was, Wells had written rather less than enough, though with a compensatory excess of distaste. But it was to this concept of power as a factor in progress, a factor as indispensable as mind, that Becker kept returning, to temper and refine his ideas in successive studies.

He had also gently chided Wells for writing history *à la Voltaire*. Still, under the mockery Becker let it be sensed that he too was a man of feeling. His expression of belief in the capacity and goodness of man was on that occasion ironic and inverted, because he himself in those years was inhibited, unsure, and not a little nihilistic in an indifferent way. Seen in retrospect, however, this intimation pointed to the future. It foreshadowed the robust faith of his last writings,

the affirmation following the embarrassed probings
that marked *Progress and Power*. In this respect too
the early essay anticipated his later writing. Meantime, the events of the next decade and a half were
ill calculated to overcome his skepticism on the score
of man's perfectibility or strengthen what little conviction remained concerning the doctrine of human
progress.

If a questioning temper was not new during the
twenties and thirties, there was ominous novelty in
the bitter and widespread rejection of the liberal
creed. A generation earlier Sorel and others had
taunted the bourgeoisie for harboring illusions of
progress, but Sorel's words while certainly echoed,
had not then taken flight. Now the deeply imbedded
irrational forces which he had helped release were
even in the land of the free and the home of democracy mischievously joined, reenforced by war and the
great depression, in their capacity for doing evil.

The limitations of the reason that Becker so greatly
cherished and cultivated with such rare distinction
had become apparent. It matters little whether it was
from William James or John Dewey, Bergson or
Freud if not Marx, or from them all or independently
of them all, that he derived and fashioned his own
views on the purposive nature of man's thinking. For

in those middle years he was reaching full maturity
as writer and thinker. Deeply introspective and rigorously honest in assessing the thinking process, he
fully agreed with Laurence Sterne that "millions of
thoughts are every day swimming quietly in the middle of the thin juice of a man's understanding without
being carried backwards or forwards till some little
gusts of passion or interest drive them to one side."
He linked this pragmatism to his much-disputed idea
of history, his famous relativist position that absolute
norms did not exist, that old views were ever being
jostled by new, that the observer for all his presumed
detachment was part of the observed. Reason, truth,
and value judgments were purely relative, having
neither objective validity nor meaning apart from the
social situation in which they were framed and from
which they arose. Long before he elaborated this
heresy in a challenging presidential address before the
American Historical Association in 1931, Becker had
solemnly apostrophized the muse with the words: "O
History, how many truths have been committed in
thy name!"

Perhaps, he had then suggested, the idea of progress
was such a truth, an illustration of the Voltairean
quip that history was a pack of tricks that we play
upon the dead, those dead whose mute and unresist-

ing aid we invoke in the realization of our own emotional peace. Since all ideas came to the surface of consciousness only for the sake of behavior, since present consciousness was linked by memory to the past while looking forward by anticipation and hope to the future, perhaps the doctrine of progress was itself only a spurious or passing truth committed in the name of history and now under altered circumstances neither useful nor tenable.

He had also been for years obsessed by the devastating implications of cosmic indifference to man. Like Pascal, whose tortured perspicuity he so deeply admired, he pointed with melancholy pride to the paradox of man triumphant over cosmos, of the thinking reed, at the very moment that the universe was crushing him in death, remaining victorious in knowing that he existed, while the universe knew nothing of him or what it was doing. The universal unawareness, this law of indifference, appears not to have upset his personal equanimity. But whatever the heavens were telling and the firmament displaying, to Becker they did not disclose the operation of natural law or the workings of a divine plan which preferred good over evil, free enterprise and liberal democracy over totalitarianism, or even the reverse. To accept cosmic indifference meant to deny a moral order with which man through his reason and his goodness could establish a harmonious understanding. Pragmatism, historical relativism, and scientific naturalism alike undermined the foundations on which the idea of progress rested.

What then? How extricate the thinking reed from the impasse in which he was caught? The spectacle of a social universe left, as Becker saw it when he was writing *Progress and Power,* to "the chance operation of individual self-interest and the unorganized pressure of mass opinion," grievously depressed him; and he found little to exhilarate him in the related conclusion that this mass intelligence functioned most effectively at the level of primitive fears and tabus.

Those were not only years of wavering faith: they were years when ill-health and pain were depleting his small store of physical energy. In those years of gloom he composed his most despondent essays: "New Liberties for Old" published in 1936 but written some years before, "Freedom of Speech" in 1934, and "Liberalism, A Way Station" in 1932. In the last named Becker touched deep bottom. The very title denoted his willingness to consider the proposition that perhaps liberty had played out its role. Superficially, man still had an option between "a ruthlessly regulated economy" and a free competitive economy "made workable by whatever patchwork of socialistic devices," but what a cruel choice was offered in inviting him to choose between liberty and equality. "Choose? Oh me, that word choose," cried Becker. "We cannot choose liberty without denouncing the drastic methods now being taken to obtain equality, or choose equality so obtained without betraying liberty." And in any case the average man who operated best on the level of primitive fears and tabus cared little enough for liberty. So little in fact that if you gave him security and within that security the liberty to do what everybody else alongside him was doing, he would probably never know or at any rate soon forget that liberty had departed. Perhaps liberalism was after all only a way station along the route that humanity had traversed, no more than a rationalization of democracy, and democracy itself only a passing phase. Perhaps, said Becker tenaciously worrying that dismal thought, the egalitarianism we were approaching would in its turn "prove to be a new rationalization, an intellectual by-product of complex, economically interdependent industrialized societies working inevitably, and no doubt impersonally towards stability and equilibrium?" [1]

[1] From "Liberalism, A Way Station," quoted in *Every Man His Own Historian* (New York, 1935), pp. 99–100.

## Introduction

Could we ourselves blot out from memory the great alarm, the deepening despondency, the near hysteria of those years, we might be tempted to suspect Becker, soul of integrity that he was, of indulging a little in histrionics, of enjoying in public the quandary in which he had encased himself. As we look back upon it, there seemed no need for his bleak dejection. *As we look back upon it* — that is the point. Becker was not looking back; he was in the thick of the night, peering anxiously through the darkness for signs of light. It was in no spirit of mock heroism that he resigned himself to an unwelcome way out of the difficulty, to a future where the solution of human problems would be imposed not by choosing between alternatives, but by accepting the pressure of common men and the rhythm of the machines they tended. He was displaying the same stoicism and the same tough common sense that he always employed. He was in fact regaining his balance.

To the extent that the world seemed to be moving toward an undifferentiated uniformity that offended cultivated tastes, the pages of *Progress and Power* are suffused with melancholy. Yet the nostalgia for intellectual and aesthetic delights which Becker saw receding into memory gives a false tone to the book. The survey of the past was after all only a device enabling him to scan the future; and the future, seen in perspective, was assured. Here then was a notable shift in emphasis. In 1932 he was deeply depressed over the cost of adjustment, reluctant even for the sake of terrestrial salvation to renounce "the idle curiosity, the mental vagabondage of the brooding, reflecting mind." In *Progress and Power* on the other hand, he was far more elated over the thought that a solution could be effected without destroying the bases of democratic living than upset over what now seemed a comparatively small toll fee to get out of his difficulties. The culture pattern he knew and loved would remain much the same in forms and institutions, even though attitudes and practices would be drastically altered. Yet for some years ill health fortified his temperament in checking enthusiasm, while his thinking, set within the circle of an intellectualized apprehension of life, withheld him from elaborating the details of the solution he had come to accept.

He was doomed for many years to a kind of apathy, compounded of emotional dejection and physical tiredness. If he did not speak in fashionable terms of being frustrated by life, he always felt a little tired. He was never entirely without some discomfort from an old stomach ailment or free from the fear that relief from pain was only a respite. He was moody; and discouragement sometimes vented itself a little sharply. Of vital, abundant energy it would be a mockery to speak. By carefully husbanding what he had, he made the most of very little, not without draining some part in an effort to conceal impatience with the more unveiled manifestations of stupidity. The mildest and most endearing of men, he suffered fools less than gladly. He was disposed also to exaggerate the differences between the sophisticated and unsophisticated levels of awareness and appreciation, because he himself moved and had his being on an unusually high level of honesty and abstraction. Cut off, too, by his own choice from the generality of men, and uncompromisingly severe with his own mental processes, he tended to fall into the error of many intellectuals and underestimate the common man's capacity to resist manipulation and not be hoodwinked.

In the beginning of his career, teaching was a painful experience for him. He suffered agonies, as he later recalled, in facing his students or even at the prospect of having to face them. By his early Cornell days, he was the joy of his admirers with the cool, detached way in which he could say "I don't know" to an ill-advised question; but few of us appreciated

at what cost this assurance had been won, how many
vigils dedicated to anticipating questions that might
be asked on the following day, how many years of
deliberate training of his memory. As time and academic renown brought him a measure of financial
security, Becker often relaxed from strain in a variety
of diversions that respectful seminar students found
hard to associate with his intellectual astringency.
Not even distance kept him from being a big league
baseball fan. For many years he played billiards at
the local Town and Gown almost with academic
regularity, as though it were a scheduled class exer-
cise, and, what was more, with almost professional
mastery. On less public occasions and for the benefit
of a few intimates he was known to compose gay and
delightful doggerel. If he loved to read novels, he
also borrowed murder mysteries in armfuls from the
lending library; and he was a devotee of the movies,
such as were shown at Ithaca. Most of all he found re-
laxation in taking the family or friends for a spin
in the new Dodge. To a sometime graduate student
greatly impressed with Becker's professorial affluence,
there seemed always to be a new Dodge. He drove
with skill, but with considerable speed too, and to an
old friend his familiar countenance, as he sat at the
steering wheel and talked, seemed curiously distorted,

one side resembling Socrates and the other, Barney Oldfield.

From his reading and thinking, from clarification of thought in conversation, even in lectures as he loved to point out, he acquired slowly over the years that grave yet kindly serenity which was his indubitable hallmark. If there were only a single word to characterize his quality, without question wisdom would be the most appropriate. Perhaps serenity is too suggestive of superiority to convey his peculiar union of pity and irony, wry humor, inner assurance and discriminating impatience. For the unfettered well-wishers of humanity, the idealists whose distress over cruelties or evils led them to vault over the high hazards of historical experience, he reserved a forbearing disapproval and a whimsical tolerance. Toward the pretentious of both sexes and all ages, and toward the officious, he entertained a fine contempt. He was no joiner of movements, and his modesty and sense of dignity of personality made him resentfully critical of any abuse of power.

On the other hand, he never had to be reminded that his humbleness was as good as anybody else's. For all his sense of futility, no Hamlet-like doubts assailed him. In his slow, quiet, and quizzically deliberate way he kept an even keel. Had Becker lived and died in

# Introduction

some small village community, he probably would
have been known and remembered locally as a fellow
with a lot of horse sense. Possibly, with his old-
fashioned rugged individualism and his absence of
affectation and vanity, with his curious insistence on
telling the truth in a simple way, he might have
achieved the distinction, not altogether invidious, of
being called a character.

Endowed with those attributes and a reflective temper that study had sharpened and refined, he found it
a challenging undertaking to write about vast sweeps
of time and trace the play of great forces. But historian of ideas (and devoted reader of novels), he knew
too much about men and women to countenance the
illusions of scientific history. He would neither con-
vert the processes of history into logical inevitabili-
ties, nor reduce man to an automatic convenience,
neatly illustrating some profound theory of behavior
or explanation of historical development. The brilliant analysis of an emotional and intellectual impasse in his early essay, "The Dilemma of Diderot,"
and the vignettes of such diverse people as Frederick
the Great, Mazzini, Rousseau, and Cavour, in *Modern History,* remind us of the delicate and sympa-
thetic awareness with which he appreciated many
facets of human personality. Without the advantage

xxvii

*Introduction*

of formal training in psychology, or of psychoanalysis as far as his friends know, he had learned to accept the casual, the contingent, and the wayward as elements of the human adventure.

Nor did philosophy ever represent to him an opportunity to escape from life and evade social responsibilities. On the contrary, he had a pronounced sense of the historian's responsibility. He held with Dewey that philosophy was a "critique of basic and widely shared beliefs." The philosopher was one who came to grips with the key problems of value in his own culture, seeking to end characteristic disturbances and mediate between divergent needs by elaborating new ideas appropriate to the occasion. This was, however, what the historian was also concerned with, if he were worth his salt. While he was discharging his specialized obligations in accordance with the canons of his craft and through a medium of expression appropriate to the particular historical problem at hand, he should still be writing history *en philosophe*. A preoccupation with values, for direction as well as for details, for ends not less than means, for the good, should permeate all his conclusions, while guiding and controlling his inquiry. Unless he knew in advance what questions he wished to put, he was working without direction, and his product might well be an abuse of the reader's confidence.

This was the sort of task that Becker set for himself when he wrote *Progress and Power*. He was bringing to consciousness in a highly intellectualized form the shocks that were troubling his age. He was propounding in the light of his specialized competence solutions for the guidance of his fellow men. And as a reader in his own turn pondered over the problems which bemused Becker, the antitheses of stability and change, harmony and conflict, appearance and reality, an impression slowly gathered that one had returned to the eighteenth century. For of Becker it should be said, as it has been said of Gibbon, that he never left the age of the enlightenment. Whatever he wrote about or wherever he was, the transplanted Iowa farm boy did not venture far from his spiritual home in Adam Smith's Edinburgh or the Paris of the *philosophes*.

A few voices may occasionally have been lifted from the side of the specialists to regret what they considered his unprofessional predilection for philosophy, but none ever contested his superb professional competence. Becker was widely recognized as a masterly craftsman and held in the highest esteem for his mag-

nificent command of a research technique that he
affected to make little of. There is nothing in the
known record challenging his devotion to truth,
though he had made it clear from a very early date
that he was happily indifferent to pursuing truth for
the sake of vindicating the hallowed rules governing
the quest. Outside of his brilliant doctoral disserta-
tion on political parties in New York on the eve of
the revolution and his *Declaration of Independence*
he did not make what is formally called an "original
contribution to learning." Becker was no savant, and
his interest in swelling the body of factual information could not be considered overwhelming. In those
circumstances the widespread recognition of his ex-
traordinary talents, which made him in his later years
a dominant force in American historiography, is a
tribute to the discrimination of his colleagues in the
field.

Personality and character, temperament and qualities of mind were all reflected in Becker's literary
style. He is a classic example of style revealing the
man. What his style does not possess is what Becker
himself lacked, a joyous, full-bodied, and colorful
sense of life. In his earlier writing, possibly because
he was still young, in good health, and not over-
burdened with doubts, he displayed a whimsy, a light-

hearted gaiety, an exuberance even, which little by
little disappeared from his later work. He was chary
of descriptive adjectives, and for adverbs of color he
seemed to entertain a positive distrust. Knowing the
man, one took it for granted that his writing should
have more line than depth and less color than rhythm.
It conveyed neither impressions of physical turmoil
nor of emotional agitation, and his smooth, flowing
legato was not often interrupted by the shock of dramatic contrasts. Elemental urges and biological impulses, when they emerged on his pages, were attired
in seemly literary dress.

Nuanced, however, graceful and full of charm his
style was, an instrument of exquisite distinction. Like
its creator it had the virtues of highest lucidity, sensi-
tivity of spirit, and unseen yet profoundly sensed
control. No invertebrate flabbiness of thought or construction marred its ordered precision, and there was
between the tempered subtlety of his mind and the
measured, often stately though informal cadence of
his words a complete and intimate rapport. An understanding amounting to fusion prevailed between
the discriminating author and the contrived under-
statement of his writing, so gravely ironic at need,
or when it served his purpose, so sharp and piercing.
The disarming and admired simplicity, while it mir-

rored his distaste for pretence and affectation, was supreme artifice brilliantly achieved, but an effortless ease purchased at the price of the same assiduous toil that enabled him to get at the heart of the matter without lacerating the delicate tissue around. Only fugitive metaphors larded bare facts, and similes rarely modified his expository bluntness. In irony and urbane wit, his style like his thoughts was rich; but biting satire was infrequent. No external application of polish achieved the effects that Becker wished to create. The matchless felicity was derived from an inner synthesis of mind and mood which imbued the best of his writing with a subdued, sustained, and almost haunting eloquence.

By the time of *Progress and Power,* Becker had reacted against misfortune, and his balance was in the main restored, but he remained ill-secure in mind over the tentative cast of his prognosis for the future. It was not his general practice to invite comment on his writing, least of all on broad, philosophical subjects, but in a letter written from Stanford on May 5, 1935, he clearly revealed his misgivings. After reporting that his lectures had been well received, he went on to say: "Now I will put them aside for a few months to get an objective view of them. . . . I am going to send one copy to you . . . if you will promise hand on heart, to give me your quite unprejudiced critical opinion. Not to praise Caesar, but if necessary to bury Caesar is what I want."

Those misgivings were in a sense well-grounded. *Progress and Power* is quintessential Becker, one of his most provocative books and certainly one of his most beautifully written. Keen and searching in its insight and fascinating for the richness that it reveals of his well-stored and allusive mind, it shows Becker in his most stimulating and tantalizing vein, holding a brilliant colloquy with himself. But it also discloses the doubts and uncertainties which beset him. In the running debate one voice seems to say: Without expecting too much from reason, man must use it, limited, contingent, purposive, for what it is worth. But we must learn to cut hopes down to size, edit for twentieth-century expectations the hopeful Tenth Epoch of Condorcet's *Esquisse*. Another voice is heard saying farewell to the old-fashioned, rationalist intellectuals who still sought to instill the spirit of brotherhood into the heart of man. It is heard crying hail to the technological elite of tomorrow, those new guides whose concern is with the needs of technical organization, who speak not the language of persuasion but express themselves in the symbols that have to do with controls and planning.

It was Becker's guarded belief that the two voices could be harmonized. To edit Condorcet would not mean abandoning the hope that our ancestors had placed in reason. It meant shifting our front, reorganizing our forces, withdrawing for the time being to a prepared position from which, under the new leadership, we would advance more securely if not more rapidly toward the old goal of peace and plenty, liberty and equality and happiness for all. It was a way of admitting that the erratic and poorly designed brains of man could not do many of the specialized tasks of today nearly so well as the superior built-in brains of the machines. As steam power had supplemented or replaced muscle, so the human brain would make place for electronics.

Becker did not live long enough to work out the implications and explore the possibilities in the vast uncharted terrain of "control and communication in the animal and the machine" — to make use of the subtitle of Norbert Wiener's exciting *Cybernetics,* where these possibilities are probed. Had he survived to investigate the subject, surely he would have been captivated by the discovery of machines that received orders, enjoyed good electronic memory and, anticipating the actions of man on the basis of his reactions as studied by mathematicians and psychologists, made decisions on their own. Here he would have found vindication for his own prediction that the fact of progress, without the sustaining idea, could most effectively be realized by leaving it to the machines. Leaving it to the machines would be one way, and not the worst, of giving man the long desired opportunity of enlisting his historical experience, his matter of fact apprehension of external nature, in the service of his social destiny. And how the paradox would have stirred Becker, that at the very moment that man gave up his initiative to take his cue from the machines which, ignoring purposes and emotions, attended strictly to the business at hand, he still had the cheerless solace of knowing that he had triumphed over them, because the machine would not know of its success nor recognize in man its victim, its designer and creator. Not the starry firmament above, nor the moral law within, would have filled Becker with wonder and awe, but man communing with nature via an electronic tube.

What he did work out in some detail was the correlated concept of control and planning. For to follow the rhythm and tempo set by the machines meant accepting responsibility to compel obedience to their needs; and this in turn meant organizing planning for the many, while jealously preserving their freedoms. This vision was Becker's New Harmony, where control-men would socialize the strategic liberties of thought and expression, learning and teaching, and all the civil liberties that under no circumstances would be sacrificed. In *Progress and Power* he only reached out for the vision; in his last books, *Modern Democracy, How* New *Will the Better World Be?*, and *Freedom and Responsibility,* he came to realize that he was doing even more than saving the strategic liberties. He was also drafting a rough blueprint for the richer culture of a socialized democracy, where the individual personality would have a greater opportunity for growth than in the planless, atomized democracy of today.

So captivated was he by his vision of democracy triumphant that he proclaimed in an exultant and moving passage that the traditional democratic values were in fact older and more universal than democracy and in no wise dependent on it. "They have a life of their own apart from any particular social system or type of civilization. They are the values which . . . men have commonly employed to measure the advance or the decline of civilization, the values they have celebrated in the saints and sages whom they have agreed to canonize. They are the values that readily lend themselves to rational justification, yet need no justification." [1]

Becker had travelled a long way from doubt. Taken literally this triumphant ode was at variance with all the thinking of his lifetime. It was Becker turned Burke in awareness of the organic unity of life and the continuity of human history. The words do not matter much, for it is the spirit that counts. It was Becker reaffirming his faith in his way of life and the way of life of his fathers. Even at his most cynical, he had always remained a believer at heart. When these last words were written he had returned to the fold. He had rejoined Voltaire and Condorcet and Wells and all the goodly company who wished humanity well.

*New York University*

[1] "Some Generalities That Still Glitter," in *The Yale Review*, XXIX (June, 1940), 666.

# Preface

THIS VOLUME CONTAINS three lectures delivered at Stanford University, on the Raymond Fred West Memorial Foundation, in April 1935. The lectures are printed as given, except for some revision at the close of the last lecture and the omission, at the beginning of each lecture, of introductory remarks appropriate in oral delivery but superfluous in a printed version. I feel a certain reluctance in publishing the lectures at all, being fully aware of the disparity between the scope of the subject and my own limited competence to give it adequate treatment. My only justification must be that I have attempted nothing more ambitious than what cartographers call a diagrammatic sketch — a diagrammatic projection of human history that makes no claim to accuracy in detail. The dates given are of course only approximate, and the generalizations, if applied to any particular historical situation, would need many qualifications. I shall be content if the general idea presented in the lectures is sufficiently relevant to merit a fuller and more discriminating treatment than I have been able to give it.

There are two points that I wish to make clear. One is that the term "power" is here used in the most gen-

eral sense: by an "expansion of human power" I
mean no more than the capacity of men to do something, whether in the mental or the physical realm,
that they could not do before. The other point is that
I have not attempted to find "causes" of historical
phenomena. I do *not* maintain that technological appliances are *primary causes* of events, or that they provide an *adequate explanation* of human progress. The
search for causes and explanations of historical events,
if these terms are to be taken in any scientific or philosophic sense, calls for a different method of approach
than that of telling the story of a particular series of
events by narration and description, which is the
method that historians have always employed and still
chiefly employ. Historians do, to be sure, find any
number of causes and explanations of particular
events — it is supposed to be their chief task. There
is no harm in that, provided it be understood that the
causes historians commonly find are of the same order
as those which we all employ, and necessarily, to facilitate ordinary human intercourse: As, for example,
the "cause" offered by Levin for being late at his own
wedding, which was that his shirts had been mislaid.
Knowing Levin, everyone concerned could understand that perfectly, and accept it as an adequate "explanation." No one, least of all Kitty, felt it necessary
to be scientific to the tiresome point of asking what

was the cause of shirts being mislaid, or what was the cause of shirts being essential to weddings anyway, still less what was the cause of weddings in general or of Levin's wedding in particular. Once you become really curious about causes you soon find yourself confronted with the electron (or whatever it is now) as the primary cause; and the electron, apart from the fact that no one knows what it really is, is of no use in explaining the phenomena that historians deal with. I take it that the "causes" of phenomena are implicit in the phenomena themselves, and are not to be identified with particular aspects of the phenomena separated out and regarded as the sole or the primary activating agencies.

This is why I do not understand those who maintain that "material interests" are the primary and "ideas" only the secondary causes of social activities, or those others who maintain the reverse of this. I do not know how men can try to satisfy material needs without first thinking about them, or how they can think about satisfying such needs unless the needs already exist. Similarly, I cannot suppose that man could have developed the intelligence he has without the implements of power his intelligence has devised, or that he could have devised the implements of power he has without an intelligence adequate to de-

## Preface

vise them. Without troubling to inquire which is more important than the other, I have therefore been content to note an apparent correlation between them — to assume that the multiplication of implements of power has at every stage in human history been as essential to the development of intelligence as the development of intelligence has been essential to the multiplication of implements of power.

The general idea of which these lectures are an elaboration was, I think, first suggested to me by a passage in J. M. Keynes' *Essays in Persuasion,* and my belief that something might be done with it was strengthened by many wide-ranging discussions with my colleague, Professor Loren Petry. The manuscript has been read by Professor Petry, Professor Leo Gershoy of Long Island University, Dr. Max Lerner, formerly of Harvard University and now with *The Nation,* and Dr. Robert R. Palmer, to all of whom I am indebted for helpful criticisms and suggestions. I wish also to express my appreciation of the many courtesies extended to me by the president, the faculty, and the students of Stanford University during my temporary residence in that most hospitable community.

CARL L. BECKER

Ithaca, New York
November 28, 1935

# Contents

*Progress and Power*

# I
# Tools and the Man

## 1

WE ARE all familiar with the word "progress." Like
any other word it has a primary meaning, which my
dictionary informs me is "to move forward." In this
sense it is merely a convenient term of reference
which one may use without becoming involved in any
metaphysical imbroglio. But, like many another innocent word, the word "progress" has taken on secondary meaning. Raised to the dignity of a noun and
charged with philosophical implications, it has long
been permitted to associate, perhaps not quite on
equal terms, with such eminent scientific words as
"process," "development," and "evolution." In this
austere company it is not to be approached lightly, or
without precautions. It is not, like "process," an entirely neutral term, or, like "development" and "evolution," one from which it is easy to eliminate all but
the faintest vestiges of ethical significance. On the
contrary, it is so heavily loaded with moral and teleo-

logical overtones that no scientist with any sense of decency will use it. It implies that there are values in the world. It implies, not only that the world moves forward, but that it moves forward to some good purpose, to some more felicitous state. In short, the word Progress, like the Cross or the Crescent, is a symbol that stands for a social doctrine, a philosophy of human destiny.

In his excellent book, *The Idea of Progress,* Professor J. B. Bury has traced the history of this social doctrine. Confined for the most part to the Western world, it is scarcely older than the seventeenth century. Francis Bacon and Pascal were among the first to declare that the ancients were not necessarily superior to the moderns. A century later Chastellux expressed the sense of his time by saying: "We have admired our ancestors less, but have thought better of our contemporaries and have expected more of our descendants"; while Condorcet undertook to prove that "the perfectibility of man is really infinite." This conclusion seemed not incredible to that optimistic age, since God was assumed to have designed the universe in such wise that man was the master of his fate: by taking thought he could always, with the assistance of the "laws of nature and of nature's God," add a cubit to his stature. The less optimistic nineteenth century discreetly rejected the word "perfectibility" in favor of the word "progress." Progress could be regarded as a gradual movement forward, as gradual as you pleased, toward an end that need not be too precisely defined. Throughout the nineteenth century, when even common men could see improvements effected day by day all about them, progress was indeed not so much a theory to be defended as a fact to be observed. In that prosperous, coal-smudged age it seemed hardly necessary for man to take thought in order to add a cubit to his stature: a cubit would obviously be added to his stature whether he took thought or not. Men had only to go about their private affairs, and something not themselves would do whatever else was necessary.

In this sense nineteenth-century social philosophers, with few exceptions, formulated the doctrine of progress. According to Hegel, the force not ourselves which would bring us to the good end of Freedom was the Absolute Idea, a kind of Universal Reason working over the heads of men, a *Vernunft* inclosing and reconciling within its cloudy recesses innumerable and conflicting *Verstände*. Classical economists maintained that a fixed Natural Order, of which one aspect was the law of individual self-interest, could be relied upon to bring about whatever happiness a harsh world held for the greatest number. The Positivists worried about the world more than they needed to, apparently, since Comte announced that the law of the three stages had already ushered in the final stage of scientific thought and material prosperity. Karl Marx, turning Hegel's Absolute Idea upside down, declared with dogmatic conviction that Dialectic Materialism, functioning through the economic class conflict, would inevitably issue in the social revolution and the establishment of a classless society. And finally (to make an end of it) Herbert Spencer demonstrated at length that the universal law of evolution, as inexorable as the law of gravitation and no less valid in the social than in the material world, was effecting a progressive, and by implication a desirable, "transformation of the homogeneous into the heterogeneous."

For two centuries the Western world has been sustained by a profound belief in the doctrine of progress. Although God the Father had withdrawn into the places where Absolute Being dwells, it was still possible to maintain that the Idea or the Dialectic or Natural Law, functioning through the conscious purposes or the unconscious activities of men, could be counted on to safeguard mankind against future hazards. However formulated, with whatever apparatus of philosophic or scientific terminology defended, the doctrine was in essence an emotional conviction, a species of religion — a religion which, according to Professor Bury, served as a substitute for the declining faith in the Christian doctrine of salvation: "The hope of an ultimate happy state on this planet to be enjoyed by future generations . . . has replaced, as a social power, the hope of felicity in another world."

Since 1918 this hope has perceptibly faded. Standing within the deep shadow of the Great War, it is difficult to recover the nineteenth-century faith either in the fact or the doctrine of progress. The suggestion casually thrown out some years ago by Santayana, that "civilization is perhaps approaching one of those long winters which overtake it from time to time," seems less perverse now than when it was made. Current events lend credit to the prophets of disaster who predict the collapse of a civilization that seemed but yesterday a permanent conquest of human reason; and this discouraging view of the facts finds adequate rationalization in old or new pessimistic theories, the most notable being that of Spengler, who has restated, in biological terminology, the ancient Greek doctrine of eternal recurrence.

Meanwhile, nineteenth-century theories of progress are, for the most part, quietly slipping into limbo.

7

Of the two that are any longer affirmed with confidence, one has been amended, the other has few adherents. A small company of Neo-Hegelians, with Benedetto Croce as its spokesman, remain confident that the Idea will see us through; but the world is in no mood to heed, even if it could understand, this survival of nineteenth-century idealism. Marxians still announce that the Dialectic's in its heaven and all's well with the world, but the latest exegetes hold that Dialectic alone is not enough: the Dialectic must be assisted by the conscious purpose of a disciplined revolutionary party employing a deliberately devised revolutionary technique. Those who formerly relied upon the beneficent operation of natural law now learn from the highest authority that their faith was misplaced. Economists who know Ricardo assure us that the natural law of individual self-interest is less likely to bring happiness than disaster to the greatest number; and the consolation, slight at any time, of knowing that we are moving from "the homogeneous to the heterogeneous" is now withdrawn, since scientists tell us that nothing is any longer certain except perhaps the law of probability.

At the present moment the world seems indeed out of joint, and it is difficult to believe with any conviction that a power not ourselves — the Idea or the Di-

alectic or Natural Law — will ever set it right. The
present moment, therefore, when the fact of progress
is disputed and the doctrine discredited, seems to me
a proper time to raise the question: What, if anything, may be said on behalf of the human race? May
we still, in whatever different fashion, believe in the
progress of mankind?

## 2

To say anything relevant to a question of this order, it is obviously desirable, first of all, to define
one's premises, to indicate one's presuppositions. Fortunately for me, the low barometer of the prevailing
climate of opinion is peculiarly favorable to the some-
what depressing assumptions which I find it necessary
to make. I shall assume that man has not the advantage of being either the cherished child of a divinity
that shapes his activities to some unknown good end,
or a safely projected reflection of an impregnable Absolute Idea, or a creature happily, if unconsciously,
designed to illustrate an economic or a biological law
of history. On the contrary, I shall assume that man
has emerged without credentials or instructions from
a universe that is as unaware of him as of itself, and
as indifferent to his fate as to its own. I shall assume
that man, like other living organisms, has had to take

9

his chances, has had to do whatever he has done at his own risk, has had to make his own way and pay his own score. I shall assume that, conditioned by his environment and his own nature, he acts solely in response to his own impulses and purposes. I shall assume that his own purposes are the only ones anywhere available; and I shall assume that his purposes, when he experiences them, seem to him valid, and that his acts, at the moment of action, seem to him good.

Having made these assumptions, I now face the crucial difficulty that always arises in any discussion of human progress — the difficulty of finding a standard for measuring it. If progress means to go forward, one naturally asks, forward to what end, to the attainment of what object? There is of course no difficulty in finding an object; the difficulty is in getting any reasonable number of people, for any reasonable length of time, to agree that the object is a valid one. If the object of this lecture is to speak for fifty minutes, I am making notable progress merely by reading one sentence after another. But you may be perverse enough to insist that the only valid object of the lecture is to clarify the subject chosen, and from that point of view some of you may think I am making progress, others not. There are still other possibilities. One of them is that the object of the lectures is to clarify a subject of importance to an academic community. From that point of view you may judge that, however successful I may be in illuminating the subject of progress, no progress is being made because the subject of progress is of no importance to an academic community. Another possibility, of which I am at this moment keenly aware, is that all lectures are an abomination. If that is so, then the establishment of the West Memorial Foundation was clearly a mistake, an unnoted incident perhaps in the decline of the capitalist system, to which you and I, befuddled by the illusion of progress, are now from moment to moment progressively contributing.

This frivolous example may serve to make vivid the difficulty of determining whether progress is a fact or an illusion. It appears to be one or the other according to the individual point of view, and the assumptions from which I start seem to make one point of view as good as another. What then is the sense of talking about human progress if we have no more stable standards of value for measuring it than the infinitely various and ever-changing judgments of individual men? Mr. G. K. Chesterton, in one of his happier moments, declares that there is no sense at all. "Nobody," he says, "has any right to use the word 'progress' unless he has a definite creed. . . . Nobody can be progressive without being doctrinal; I might almost say that nobody can be progressive without being infallible — at any rate, without believing in some infallibility. For progress by its very name indicates a direction; and the moment we are doubtful about the direction, we become to the same degree doubtful about the progress." On this account of it, we can all easily recognize Mr. Chesterton's right to talk about progress, since he has the courage to be doctrinal: he may not be infallible, but at least he manages, every bright morning, to convey the impression of having recently and pleasantly communed with some infallibility.

Unfortunately, few of us, historians and social theorists, have Mr. Chesterton's courage to be doctrinal. We do not really believe in any infallibility. Must we then cease to talk about progress? I think Mr. Chesterton is right to this extent: unless we can recover faith in some infallibility, we should cease, if not to talk about progress, at least to talk about it as a movement toward some known good end. To choose either alternative is not easy — at least for those who wish to be at once scientific and uplifting. As scientists we abjure infallibility, but without some plausible imitation of it we find it difficult to bring spiritual first aid

12

to a harassed and perplexed generation. The word "progress" still symbolizes the persistent desire of men (and historians and social theorists are men too — it is perhaps our chief merit) to find something that is and will forever remain good. That is no doubt why, without believing in any infallibility, we still seek, in the half-wrecked doctrine of progress, securities that only infallibility can provide. Our behavior is not unlike that of certain Protestant sects whose habit of going to church has outlived their religious convictions: we have made a fair recovery from the Absolute, but its after-effects linger in our emotions, like an irritating cough in the bronchial tubes after influenza.

If historians appear not to suffer from the after-effects of the Absolute Idea, that is chiefly because they make such a point of not having any ideas at all, of being strictly objective and letting "the facts speak for themselves." Nevertheless, although we do not use the word "progress," the subtle implications of the idea are in our writings — we contrive to make the facts speak for themselves in that sense. Sociologists are more brazen than historians, or perhaps only more courageous. They openly profess to be interested in ideas; and we find some of them using the word "progress," and looking for standards of value, or as they prefer to say, "criteria," for measuring it. They find a good many criteria, necessarily so perhaps, since even by their own account of it no one is satisfactory. Among the criteria presented for consideration are the following: Happiness, Longevity, Material Well-Being, Intelligence, Morality. What can be said for these criteria as standards for measuring the progress of mankind toward a good end?

I think that very little can be said for them. Happiness is surely incommensurable, and no one but the sad-faced Utilitarians ever thought of making so illusive a quality the basis of a social theory. Longevity is at least measurable; but, apart from the fact that vital statistics from the time of the Neanderthalers are said to be incomplete, long life is of no value unless the life itself is satisfying. Material well-being is good, but even the Marxians do not claim that it is more than a means to something better. Intelligence? Well, yes; but intelligence for what? Intelligence is a specialized quality, specific for the task; and how can we tell whether the intelligence of Einstein is better or worse than that of Aristotle? As for morality, what, if anything, is it but custom, which is admittedly nothing if not infinitely variable?

All these criteria are empty words until we give them a content, and if they are to serve as standards of

value what content can we give them but the temporary and conflicting values of our own time? There is
of course no question as to the validity of these values
for us and for our time; and so long as they remain
values for us it is right, necessary indeed, that we
should endeavor to make them prevail. I myself recognize certain values which I endeavor to make prevail — with limited success it must be said in view of
the victorious onset, at the present moment, of alien
ideas throughout the world. The values I most cher-
ish do not thrive well in the market place or on the
"social front." They are roughly symbolized (as
ideals, be it understood, not as descriptions of fact) by
the words Liberty, Equality, Fraternity, Humanity,
Toleration, Reason. I have a profound aversion from
all that is implied (again in the light of what is desirable, not of what may be necessary) by the words
Authority, Compulsion, Obedience, Regimentation,
Uniformity, Standardization; a profound disbelief in
the virtue of solutions effected by non-rational means,
by physical force or the pressure of emotion in mass
formation. I should like as well as anyone to believe
that the universe is on the up and up and on my side;
and by recreating the world in the image of my private values and aversions I could easily present you
with a most consoling definition of human progress.

Recreating the world in my own image is, however, what I wish particularly to avoid doing — at least in so far as it can be avoided. Mankind, taking it by and large, has as yet paid so little attention to my values and aversions that it seems presumptuous to erect them into absolute standards for judging it; and it is therefore futile, for me at least, to inquire whether the human race is moving toward either a good or a bad end until some less fallible intelligence than mine turns up to tell me what that end is. Scientists, to be sure, do tell us, and with a certain air of infallibility, that there will be an end, some undetermined billions of years hence, when "the whole temple of man's achievements must inevitably be buried beneath the debris of a universe in ruins." That would be an end, sure enough, and from the point of view of omniscience perhaps a good one, the very best maybe. But we are not omniscient, and from the point of view of our finite aspirations, our limited aims, such an end is neither good nor bad, but only too remote to be practically relevant. No immediate precautions are called for, no preparations need yet be made for this last and most disastrous of all the depressions. Relatively speaking, there is time enough: time enough for man to find Utopia and live in it for a billion years, which would no doubt be sufficient to prepare him spiritually for ultimate extinction and quiescence. Even so, we do not know what this intervening, brief Utopia of a billion years might turn out to be like: we can only guess, with a degree of confidence, that we should be no more at ease in it than, shall we say, the Cro-Magnons would be in the advanced and advancing civilization of New York and Moscow.

By this indirect route I arrive at a tentative answer to the question: What can be said on behalf of the Human Race? Judged by my private values, very little can be said in its behalf: judged by the private values current at any time, the Human Race must be mostly wrong and thoroughly perverse. The answer is adequate for those who can find some infallibility — the Absolute Idea, the Dialectic, Natural Law — to set all right at the Judgment Day or in Utopia. The infallible validation of their interests and grudges, their hopes and aspirations, by setting them in a class apart, provides them with a cheap ticket to salvation: the price is merely that they should dismiss to oblivion the great majority for failing to enter their clean but sparely furnished Heaven. It is just because I cannot count on any such dressing up or dressing down of mankind that this easy answer leaves me distressed, very much so. I have not the advantage of belonging to a class apart; and since I belong to the Human

Race, I wish to think well of it — as well as possible. To think well of the Human Race I must find a place in it for those who are not of my opinion — for the Cro-Magnons; for the ferocious Assyrians; for the Egyptians, who thought it worth while to build the Great Pyramid as a tomb for King Khafra; for Messrs Hitler and Stalin; for the dwellers in the coming Utopia: none of whom, I feel sure, would sufficiently understand my values to grasp the high significance, for example, of Stanford University, or of the three lectures now being given on the Raymond Fred West Memorial Foundation!

I thus conclude that my ethical and moral judgments are, as Justice Holmes said of Truth, no more than "the system of my limitations." In the realm of practical activities I cannot transcend these limitations, but in the conceptual realm of thought I can ignore them. I will therefore, for the purpose of this discussion, dismiss all ethical and moral judgments, forget about the final or relatively good end toward which man may be moving, and endeavor to estimate human progress in terms of what man has in fact done, and of the means that have enabled him to do it, without prejudice to the values which, at any moment of time, may have seemed to him valid grounds for his activities. By taking a sufficiently long-time view of these activities, it may be possible to note in what essential respects man has become different from what he was, from his cousins the apes — those friendly enemies with whom, in "the dark backward and abysm of time," he associated on scarcely more than equal terms. The extent and character of this difference, whether the difference itself is to be judged good or ill, will be taken as the measure of human progress.

3

For taking this long-time view of human activities we are not well placed. Standing here and now, in the shadow of the Great War, events occurring here and now are seen as "close-ups," while events occurring elsewhere or in the remote past, if seen at all, are unduly foreshortened. We ought, therefore, to betake ourselves to a point in time-space from which we can look down upon the human scene with some measure of that detachment which Renan attributed to the inhabitants of Mars — and to historians! Fortunately, it is not altogether impossible to do this. One of the tricks man has picked up on his way is the power to hold himself at arm's length in order to observe himself as an object from the outside. By an imaginative flight we may take our stand anywhere in the compre-

19

hended universe, in order to observe ourselves functioning, at a particular time and place, in relation to
our fellows and to the generations of men before us.
Where then shall we place ourselves? We must be near
enough to discern the course of human history at a
glance and in its main outlines, but sufficiently removed not to be startled by the form and pressure of
particular events. A proper place, I have thought,
would be the Olympian Heights where the Greek
Gods lived: the Greek Gods were near enough to observe the activities of men, yet far enough removed to
take an objective view of their fate. We will therefore
make this imaginative flight to the Olympian Heights.
Looking down from this cool retreat, the present sad
state of the world leaves us unmoved; the Great War
seems to us no more tragic than the sack of Rome by
the Visigoths, the collapse of the capitalist system no
more significant than the extinction of the Cro-Magnons. For we are on Oympus, observing the Earth
Children whose fate we do not share, and whose activities, displayed before us along a limited Time-Scale,
we can see in part only, as a sequence of events broken
at both ends — the earliest events not visible, the latest not yet enacted.

What is the length of the Time-Scale along which
human history lies spread out before us? Anthropolo-

gists tell us that man has lived on the earth a million years, or perhaps two million, unless it should turn out to be ten million. The difference is negligible. A million years is but as a day in the sight of an anthropologist! It doesn't matter to us either, since we are concerned only with the time during which something may be known about man's activities. We will therefore begin the Time-Scale with the oldest known remains which anthropologists are willing to identify as possibly human. At present these are the skull-cap, teeth, and thighbone uncovered in Java which we are told must have been deposited there about 500,000 years ago. Since the date is only approximate, we will extend it by the inconsiderable trifle of 6,000 years, the period of recorded history, the period during which men have lived under civilized as distinct from primitive conditions. Thus human history, as we from Olympus look down upon it, runs from the Java Man to Mussolini — or Roosevelt; and the Time-Scale is 506,000 years.

The term Java Man is of course only a loose, popular designation. Anthropologists, with commendable caution in drawing inferences from fragmentary remains, identify the creature by the term *Pithecanthropus erectus* — Erect-Ape-Man. Nothing could suit our purpose better than to be permitted to begin human history with a creature that cannot be differentiated with assurance from the apes. The present races of men, it is true, are not supposed to be lineally descended from the Java Man, but their remote ancestors, if we could find their remains (in central Asia perhaps?) would almost certainly turn out to be Erect-Ape-Men too. We will therefore imitate the mathematicians by introducing a fiction into our historical equation, a quite correct scientific procedure if we remember and allow for the fiction. Making allowance for this fiction then, the Java Erect-Ape-Man provides us with a point of reference for noting the difference, such as it is, between man at the beginning and man at the end of the Time-Scale.

At the beginning of the Time-Scale men and apes are hardly distinguishable. The Erect-Ape-Men appear to have neither articulate speech, nor traditions, nor accumulated knowledge. They have few means of defense or aggression except the physical force of their bodies and the instinctive aptitudes provided by their biological inheritance. To us they appear to be associating and contending with the apes on fairly equal terms. But if we turn to the end of the Time-Scale (April 23, 1935), we can see at once that something has happened: nothing to the apes but something to

man. The apes look and behave at the end of the
Time-Scale very much as they did at the beginning:
during 506,000 years they have repeated their activities instead of extending them. But man at the end of
the Time-Scale is not what he was at the beginning.
He no longer contends and associates with his cousins the apes. He puts them in the Zoo. And if, some
fine morning, he should encounter his ancestor *Pithecanthropus* on University Avenue, he would no
doubt, failing to recognize the old man, put him in
the Zoo also. Imagine then some descendant of *Pithecanthropus* standing in the Zoo, looking up at his remote ancestor in the cage. In what essential respects
do they appear to differ? As biological specimens they
appear to us not too unlike; and if the man finds the
antics of *Pithecanthropus* amusing, it is chiefly because they parody his own on the less formal occasions
of life. If the man should be suddenly whisked to the
beginning of the Time-Scale and dropped, naked and
without appliances, among his ancestors in Java, the
amusement, if any, would not be his. All the biological progress of 506,000 years would lead him swiftly
to the final, good or bad, end of extinction. Fortunately for the man, he is not at the beginning but at
the end of the Time-Scale, in the Zoo, looking up at

*Pithecanthropus* with amusement. The reason he can afford to be amused is a simple one: he is on the outside of the cage, *Pithecanthropus* is on the inside.

All that has happened to man in 506,000 years may be symbolized by this fact — at the end of the Time-Scale he can, with ease and expedition, put his ancestors in cages: he has somehow learned the trick of having conveniently at hand and at his disposal powers not provided by his biological inheritance. *From the beginning of the Time-Scale man has increasingly implemented himself with power.* Had he not done so, he would have had no history, nor even the consciousness of not having any: at the end of the Time-Scale he would still be (if not extinct) what he was at the beginning — *Pithecanthropus erectus,* the Erect-Ape-Man. Without power no progress.

Power! I now recall that force and compulsion were listed among the words that symbolize my private aversions. It does not disturb me. Since I am no longer burdened with the task of setting the world right, it is of no significance that one of my private aversions, disguised as power, should now turn up to play a major role in the drama of human progress. The significant fact is that the human race, so far from having any aversion from power, has at all times welcomed it as a value to be cherished. Look where

24

## Tools and the Man

we will along the Time-Scale, we see men eagerly seeking power, patiently fashioning and tenaciously grasping the instruments for exerting it, conferring honor upon those who employ it most effectively. Implements of power once used may become obsolete, the secret of their use may be lost for a time; but in general it is true that once possessed of a new implement of power men do not voluntarily abandon it. Regarding it as in itself good, they use it in whatever ingenious ways it can be used, for whatever ends may at the moment seem desirable, never doubting that the desired ends will sufficiently justify the means employed to attain them.

Tools and the Man! Long ago Francis Bacon noted with precision and brevity that human intelligence and implements of power are correlated conditions of progress.

Neither the naked hand nor the understanding left to itself can effect much. It is by instruments and helps that the work is done. . . . Human knowledge and human power meet in one.

At this point a philosopher, if there be one among us, may ask which of these two factors functions as *cause* — the instruments and helps, or the intelligence that devises and uses them? The reply is that as historians we cannot find causes; we can only observe

25

events and note their correlation. At the beginning of the Time-Scale human knowledge and human power are already conjoined. The hand of *Pithecanthropus* is not entirely naked, his understanding not altogether unassisted. His hand grasps an edged flint; the look and feel of it stimulate his mind to unaccustomed activity. Which is cause, which is effect, we do not know. The first Ape-Man to learn that an edged flint could be used for cutting may have learned this momentous truth because he was more intelligent than his fellow-apes or he may have become more intelligent than his fellow-apes because his more flexible hand enabled him to verify this momentous truth. We note the correlation, and we note that it holds throughout the Time-Scale: the expansion of human intelligence appears to be as much conditioned by the multiplication of implements of power as the multiplication of implements of power is conditioned by the expansion of human intelligence.

Our first hasty glance thus discloses to view a sequence of activities that appear to be conditioned by two correlated movements — the expansion of intelligence and the multiplication of implements of power. As historians we cannot resist the temptation to divide this sequence of events into "periods," and our first impulse of course is to divide it into Ancient,

## Tools and the Man

Medieval, and Modern. This impulse we must ruthlessly control. Since our object is not to write history, but to learn something about human progress, we must look for such "periods" as may be suggested by the expansion of intelligence and the multiplication of implements of power that appear to be the correlated conditions of progress. And first of all we need to look more attentively at the implements of power themselves, in order, as it were, to locate them on the Time-Scale.

"Implements of power" is a loose but convenient shorthand phrase to denote all the *sources* of power, and all the *instruments* for exerting power, which men have discovered or invented and used for doing things which they could not do, or not so well, without them: the "instruments and helps," as Bacon said, without which "neither the naked hand nor the understanding left to itself can effect much." *Pithecanthropus* is of course himself a source of power, physical and mental; his hand and his vocal organs are instruments for exerting power. The stone in his hand is also an instrument for exerting power, but it did not come with his biological set-up: it is an "extra" which he has added to his f.o.b. equipment. We are concerned with these extras which man has added to his native endowment. The chief sources of

power which man has added to his native endowment
appear, along the Time-Scale, roughly in the following order: gravitation, fire, domestic animals, planted
seeds, water, air, magnetic force, artificial explosives,
steam, gas, electricity, radiation. The instruments for
exerting power are far more numerous than the
sources of power. At the beginning of the Time-Scale
we see *Pithecanthropus* grasping an edged flint; at the
end of it we see, in the Pennsylvania Station in New
York, a door politely opening at the request of an
"electric eye." In between are all the innumerable
hand tools, weapons, utensils, machines, machine
tools, gadgets, and appliances that man has ever used
for defense or aggression, for promoting his ease and
comfort, for the release of his emotions, for the gratifi-
cation of his intellectual curiosity and the satisfaction
of his aesthetic impulses. It is impossible to enumer-
ate them all, unnecessary even to dispose of them in
logical categories. We observe merely that the order
in which they appear on the Time-Scale is roughly determined by the sources of power available: a baked-
clay pot does not appear before men have learned to
control fire; a steam engine is not invented before
men have discovered the expansive force of steam.

This being the order in which implements of power
appear on the Time-Scale, at what points do they first

Tools and the Man

tling, at conveniently uniform intervals? Alas, no!
What we see at once, and most clearly, is that for the
first 450,000 years nothing at all appears except a few
crude hand tools. Then we see men using fire; and
after that, very gradually, better and more varied
tools make their appearance; and, finally, during the
last ten thousand years of the Time-Scale, an ever-
increasing crowd of implements of power come rushing in, like latecomers at a theater, as if fearful that all
the available places may be occupied. Nearly all the
implements of power that man has ever used are to be
seen uncomfortably huddled together well toward the
end of the Time-Scale; and if we depend upon them
to suggest periods into which the sequence of events
may be divided, it is obvious that the periods will be
very unequal in length.

Do the implements of power in fact suggest any periods into which the sequence of events may be divided? They will not "speak for themselves," but with
a little prompting they may tell us something. Since
we wish to correlate progress with the expansion of
human power and intelligence, the best plan is to
look for those discoveries or inventions that have
been followed by a marked change in man's activities
and way of living. The discovery of fire is certainly

one of these; the invention of writing is another. For a third we might take the invention of the steam engine; but since our last period ought to be long enough to turn around in at least, it will be better to take an earlier discovery — the discovery of magnetic force (China, A.D. 1160?). These three events give us four periods which may be bracketed along the Time-Scale within very roughly approximate dates.

The first period comprises the first 450,000 years — a little less than nine-tenths of the entire Time-Scale: the period when man had to make shift with a few crude hand tools. The second period comprises the next 50,000 years — a little less than one-tenth of the Time-Scale: the period when men learned to use fire, to improve their tools, weapons, utensils, to raise cereals, to domesticate animals, to weave coarse cloth, to construct shelters — the period of settled if primitive community living. The third period comprises the 5,000 years following the invention of writing — a little less than one one-hundredth of the Time-Scale: the period when men organized powerful states and empires, perfected the mechanic and the fine arts, and created by abstracting from the world disclosed to the senses, ideal conceptual realms of religion, ethics, philosophy, history, mathematics. The fourth period comprises — we know not what, since it is not yet completed. It has run a scant 1,000 years, but we can see that it is characterized by the discovery of new sources and implements of power which are enabling man to begin the deliberate and systematic mastery of the physical world, and to become increasingly aware of himself as an animated and conscious bit of cosmic dust emerging from the universe at a particular point in space and functioning there for a brief moment in cosmic time. These are the four periods, and their duration along the Time-Scale is roughly indicated by the fractions 9/10, 1/10, 1/100, and 1/500 + $x$ ($x$ being an unknown number of years to come).

It thus turns out that the periods are of unequal duration. But we can see a certain method in this madness: the periods become successively shorter. Is this because we have arbitrarily chosen to make them so? I think not. Other dividing points might indeed have been found — for example, the discovery of agriculture instead of the use of fire, the invention of the steam engine instead of the discovery of magnetic force. Nevertheless, the choices offered are limited; and the periods chosen, in so far as they do conform to certain notable changes in man's activities and way of living, become successively shorter, not because we have arbitrarily made them so, but because there is an observed correlation between two accelerated movements — the acceleration of man's capacity to discover new sources and implements of power, and the acceleration of his capacity to extend his activities and modify his way of living. The length of the periods is in inverse proportion to man's capacity to do things that he could not do before, in inverse proportions to his capacity to differentiate himself from the original Erect-Ape-Men — in short, in inverse proportion to human progress measured by this differentiation.

Thus human history, taken in at a single glance from remote Olympus, discloses itself to us a diagrammatic projection, which may be represented by two divergent lines: a straight base line which represents the Time-Scale of 506,000 years, and also the dead level of unchanging activities which would have been man's history had he been incapable of implementing himself with power; a second line, representing the extension of man's activities and power, which starts from the base line at the beginning of the Times-Scale, rises from it ever so slightly for nine-tenths of its length, and then diverges in an ever more sharply ascending curve to the end. We must now look more attentively at the sequence of events, in each of the four periods, in the hope of recognizing the types of activity that are symbolized by this diagrammatic projection. As good historians we will naturally adhere strictly to the chronological order, and begin with the first period.

## II

# The Sword and the Pen

*The generations pass away,*
*While others remain.*

ANCIENT EGYPTIAN LOVE SONG

1

THE ACTIVITIES of man during the first and by far the most extended of the four periods need not detain us long. Since the duty of the historian is to "exhaust the sources of information," the consciousness of having made an "original contribution to knowledge" is likely to be in inverse proportion to the wealth of information at his disposal. We can thus be fairly certain of the activities of *Pithecanthropus* and his descendants for 450,000 years, because we cannot see what they were doing: we can only see some fragment of skeleton remains and a few chipped-flint hand tools. The examination of these, undisturbed by other perverse intruding facts in the vast empty surrounding void, enables us to perceive, according to Mr. Gerald Heard, that the Erect-Ape-Men (Trial-Men, Dawn-Men, Sub-Men) originally lived in trees. We can, he thinks, also see them becoming "too heavy for the branches, a fall was too serious. So Nature furled their tails and . . . launched them from the leafy stocks . . . to set out on their annexation of the earth." *

In accomplishing this ambitious task, the first 450,-000 years were the hardest. One reason is that *Pithecanthropus* and his descendants did not know that Nature had launched them from the leafy stocks for purposes of her own. When a Piltdown Man or a Neanderthaler chipped a flint he was contributing to the progress of mankind, but was himself quite unaware of the fact: he was aware that he was chipping a flint. Even with the chipped flint added to his naked hand the all-absorbing object in life was to remain alive — to preserve life by outwitting the others and to sustain it by foraging for daily food. The engaging Dawn-Men were all pure extraverts: their attention was necessarily fixed upon the immediately surrounding outer world, their interest necessarily confined to the present moment. Not being securely inclosed in a padded room, their recollections of times past, like their anticipation of times to come, were such only as

* The Emergence of Man (London, 1931) , p. 28.

might be prompted by the stimulus of momentarily changing impulses, fears, and appetites. Their spatial universe was bounded by what the eye could compass, their time world scarcely more than an enduring, undifferentiated *now*. They did what the impulse of the moment commanded, and every act carried its own justification since it could not be compared, for purposes of appraisal, with any model of itself — neither with acts done and recalled from the past, nor with acts conceived and projected into the future. The Dawn-Men were anachronistic disciples of Walter Pater: for 450,000 years they "burned with a hard gemlike flame," giving the highest quality to the moment as it passed, and merely for that moment's sake. Apart from the immense initial achievement involved in the invention of hand tools, their contribution to progress was therefore slight: like their cousins the apes, they were condemned for the most part to repeat their activities, having such very limited implements with which to extend them.

Turning now to the Second Period — compared with the first no more than a brief span of 50,000 years — we note at once that man is rapidly modifying his way of living. At first we dimly discern small isolated groups of men sociably huddled around fires, perhaps at the openings of caves to which they retreat for shelter or defense, and from which they emerge, with increasingly better and more diversified tools, to hunt for food. They appear to be capable of articulate speech, and to be unconsciously submitting to a leader. Millennium after millennium slips away, and at last we note a certain concentration, a greater density of population: larger and not necessarily isolated groups permanently settled at particular places, keeping a few domestic animals, raising sparse crops of barley, cooking their food, adroitly shaping clay pots, weaving coarse cloth, constructing permanent shelters. Self-sufficing societies these are, behaving in ways that are strangely familiar to us: societies of men and women bound together by common needs and possessions, following an accepted routine of daily life, imposing upon the young and the recalcitrant conformity to immemorial custom, performing with steadfast minds and loyal hearts the unchanging necessary ritual. These creatures have so far advanced beyond the status of *Pithecanthropus* that our anthropologist will discharge them from bail and admit them to the immunities of "true men." Man the tool-using animal has emerged as man the political animal. Aristotle, were we so fortunate as to have him with us, would judge them to be neither above nor below humanity.

The creatures we are observing would not understand Aristotle. They do not know that they are men, since no one has yet created the conceptual realm in which Humanity dwells. Yet they have made the preliminary effort essential to the creation of that rarefied realm: they have enlarged the little world of Here and Now in which *Pithecanthropus* was confined. Their implements of power burden them with possessions that cannot be accommodated, with activities that cannot be effectively performed, in so small a world. Planting and harvest, the care of animals, the daily routine of household economy, and burial places of recent unforgotten dead — all these tie them to one place and require them to keep in mind their receding yesterdays and to take thought for their oncoming tomorrows. Imperceptibly, unconsciously, the confining walls of Time and Space have been pushed back a little: the spatial universe is measured by the country any man has explored and can contrast with the familiar places of daily life; the temporal universe is measured by oral tradition — the capacity of the oldest erudite bard to make vivid and to perpetuate the recollection of what is memorable.

This enlarged world does not exist apart from the expanding intelligence that made it possible. It is an artificial construction composed of diverse things in fixed relations. It is composed of men and their possessions; of the relation of men to each other and to their possessions; of the relation of men and their possessions to the outer world of Nature and to events recalled from the past and projected into the future. The task of holding this construction together lays a heavy burden on the mind, and thereby has a sobering effect. Condemned to remember and to anticipate, the creatures we are observing have not the insouciant spontaneity of *Pithecanthropus.* It is not enough for them to think of one thing at a time, or for the moment only: it is necessary for them to think of many things at the same time, and to hold them in mind as a system of enduring relations. Having created this system of enduring relations, man is himself imprisoned within it; and since he cannot escape, he must endeavor to understand it as a going concern.

The men who must grasp this system of enduring relations, being required to think of many things at the same time, learn to distinguish and to infer. They distinguish men from animals, the living from the dead, living creatures from physical objects, physical objects or living creatures subdued to men's uses from objects or influences beyond their control. To us it appears that they distinguish imperfectly and often infer incorrectly. We note that they best understand the objects of familiar use — tools, utensils, weapons, seeds, the not unfriendly animals that move and eat and sleep, and die, as men do. Any man may indeed be much attached to a particular weapon or tool, being convinced that a peculiar virtue (*mana*, power, luck) resides within it. Yet what appears most striking is that the creatures we are observing have in general "true," matter-of-fact knowledge of certain useful objects: of the uses of an axe or a handful of seeds their knowledge is durable, capable of being transmitted from generation to generation without ever having to be unlearned. Should we transport one of these creatures to the end of the Time-Scale and give him an axe or a bag of seeds, he would know what to do with them, and no one of his remote descendants would regard his behavior as strange and unaccountable.

Yes, man already knows what to do with seeds — they are to be planted in the ground. But he has learned by sad experience that seeds sometimes grow well, at other times indifferently or not at all. Seeds, like people, are perverse or perversely controlled. There are those who believe them amenable to suggestion, and in fact it has been observed that imitating the movement of growing stalks of grain by jumping high in the air has been followed by good crops.

But the more credible theory was hit upon when some alert mind noted that seeds scattered upon freshly dug graves grew better than seeds scattered elsewhere. The inference was obvious: to insure a good harvest someone must die and be buried. It was reasonable to suppose that the earth should demand something in exchange for its bounty; and so every year, at seed time, if no victims captured from alien tribes are available, young or old men volunteer or are conscripted to die in order that the harvest may be plentiful. The sacrifice is made in accordance with a fixed ritual appropriate to the solemnity of the occasion; and the chosen ones are regarded, and perhaps regard themselves, as persons apart, worthy of the high honor accorded to those who give their lives for the welfare of the community. No one doubts the wisdom of what is done: it has always been known that seeds planted in the earth will grow; it has always been known that they will grow more abundantly if the earth is propitiated by the sacrifice of human life.

The earth is not alone in calling for attention. The sun and the moon, wind and rain, rushing waters at flood, the repeated drama of night and day and the leisurely procession of the seasons — all these are obvious influences bringing good and evil to men. Fortunately, there are known ways of propitiating or out-

witting them — the practical art of Tabu, the related
science of Magic, Sorcery, and Divination, the attentive observance of custom prescribed by experience.
Since no act is indifferent, many are forbidden, while
those permitted have their appropriate time and place
and prescribed form. Since no object is necessarily in-
ert, one must strive to avoid those that may be harm-
ful, while cherishing those in which virtue resides —
those to be always carried on the person, or others of
greater potency that the Medicine Man has in his
bundle. The outward world of Nature is not something apart, indifferent to man. It is something in
whose activities men must share. One dances for joy
when the fruitful rains come; the fruitful rains will
be more disposed to come if everyone dances for joy.
The procession of the seasons, the fruition of crops,
the succession of states in the life of man from birth
to manhood, from manhood to old age, from old age
to death, from death to the continuing life thereafter
— all these are dramatic offerings in which the community must participate, according to an elaborate
unchanging ritual, to the end that the community
may be identified with the influences (Totem, Moira,
Gods, God) that make life abundant, and dissociated
from the influences (mischance, illness, famine, death)
that make it sterile. Men have learned to distinguish

and to infer; but since it is a multiplicity of concrete things, of concrete powers, that they distinguish, it is to a multiplicity of concrete actions, defined in the ritual, that their inferences lead them. In such a world, composed of a multiplicity of concrete items, all equally real and equally obvious, there is neither mystery nor miracle, nor ground for doubt, nor occasion for experiment.

Surveying human activities during the Second Period of the Time-Scale, it is obvious to us that man has greatly extended his power and modified his way of living since the day when *Pithecanthropus* was "launched from the leafy stocks to set out on his annexation of the earth." But the creatures we are observing would be disheartened indeed if we should congratulate them on having discovered a revolutionary technique for doing things that their ancestors could not do. The revolution has been so slowly accomplished that no generation of men contributing to it is aware that any essential change has taken place. The idea of progress has therefore not occurred to them. Progress itself would alarm them if they were aware of it; if aware of it they would prevent it if they could. Everything that is is to them as if it had always been, everything that they do is as if it had always been done: the memory of the oldest and the

wisest runneth not to the contrary. We thus note a
significant fact: the power of man has been extended
by limiting the freedom of men. The individual is
imprisoned in society: he can no longer respond spon-
taneously to his own momentarily changing impulses;
he must respond to impulses elicited and disciplined
by the complicated rhythm of group activities that are
themselves stabilized and validated by the impregnable convictions that to depart from customary ways is
to invite disaster. Tradition — the carrying over of
the past into the present — has made progress possible only to become a dead hand closing the door to
fruitful innovation.

As we turn away from the Second Period we note
that Time is running short — a mere 6,000 years to
come. In 500,000 years man has done what he could
with the implements of power at his disposal. Is it
likely that he will do much that is new and strange in
the few, swiftly fleeting years that remain? He will as-
suredly do little more unless he can transcend the sti-
fling static world of primitive experience in which he
is confined. Among the diverse conditions that must
unite to bring this about, one is indispensable — the
art of writing, the written record which, by providing
man with a transpersonal memory, will disclose to his
view, for discrimination and appraisal, the mythical

44

and the historic past, the familiar and the alien custom, the world as experienced and the world as
ideally conceived.

2

Our apprehensions as to man's capacity to do something new and strange all vanish as soon as we turn to
the Third Period — 5,000 years along the Time-Scale
from the invention of writing to the discovery of magnetic force. The anthropologists may lose interest, but
the historian notes with approval that within this
brief space the activities of men take on those diverse
qualities of intellectual discrimination, of ruthless action, and of unstable splendor that put him at his
ease. Displayed to view, in bold relief, are civilizations
so familiar as to seem, in contrast to the dim world
of the prehistoric, commonplace and contemporary.
Open to his inspection, in ever-increasing number,
are the blest "documentary sources," his beloved
names and dates; so that he can identify the particular
group, and in due time even the particular individual — for example, King Hammurabi, whose jaw-
bone it is needless to look for or to measure, since he
can read the code of laws, inscribed on a monolith,
which the king prepared for the better control of his
people. To the historian it is a great satisfaction to re-

alize that he is at last within the safe confines of recorded history.

Surveying the Third Period as a whole, we note that the increasing use of written records occurs only among certain groups of men in certain places — in Western Asia, Egypt, China and India, the Aegean and the Mediterranean countries, and (very late in the Third Period) in western Europe. We note also that it is in these places only that there occurs a striking extension of man's activities and powers, and that this extension is roughly in proportion to the increased use and perfection of written records. Which came first, which was "cause," which "effect," we cannot determine: the extension of man's activities in certain more densely populated regions doubtless created a peculiar need for written records in the first place, the increased use of written records doubtless facilitated the further extension of man's activities. We merely note the general fact: where the art of writing does not exist, or exists in a rudimentary form only, man's powers and way of living retain their primitive character; it is only where the art of writing develops that man emerges from the primitive to the civilized state.

That the art of writing was a discovery of crucial importance is obvious to us, but not to those who discovered it. Written records slip into the primitive convention so unobtrusively that the men who first use them are unaware of having in hand a new and revolutionary implement of power. The art of writing was not strictly speaking an invention, but rather the transformation of an old into a new magic. If we return for a moment to note the activities of primitive men, we see them making pictures. We can see, for example, a Cro-Magnon scratching, on the wall of a cave, a wonderfully accurate picture of a buffalo. Presently we see the artist scratching a second picture over the first one. This curious procedure disconcerts us until we realize that the artist may be making the picture, not primarily to satisfy an aesthetic impulse, but to assist his companions in the hunt. The virtue is not in the picture but in the execution of it: the execution is a dramatic rehearsal, a visual and muscular anticipation of the capture of a buffalo. In the course of time this excellent "art" declines; the pictures become smaller, less accurate, no more than conventional symbols. Certain alert minds, by a great effort of intelligence, realize that the picture may be taken as a visual idea of the object, or of an event symbolized by it. Early in the Third Period we can thus see an Egyptian peasant making, on the wall of his mud hut, a crude picture of a basket with some marks beside it. He does not know that he is making a notable contribution to human progress; he knows only that he is doing something that will enable him to be certain how many measures of grain he had paid in taxes, and so avoid being cheated by his tribal chief. We can see, what he could not, that he is making a written record that will enable him to verify a historical event and so avoid being cheated by his own or another's fallible recollection of it. He is transforming the old magic into a new and more potent one, the magic of the written record — a new mental tool which increases the power of his mind as formerly the flint hatchet increased the power of his hand. The function of this new tool is just this: it provides men with an artificially extended and verifiable memory of objects and events not present to sight or recollection.

Equipped with this artificial memory, men are able, other favorable conditions concurring, to do many things that could not be done before. Attending first to their outward activities, we note that they can unite small communities into large states, and by the conquest and consolidation of many states create great empires. The process is slow for the first two thousand years, but appears to accelerate thereafter. On the lower Euphrates little communities are united into the kingdom of Sumer and Akkad; Sumeria is presently absorbed in a larger Babylonia; Babylonia in a larger Assyria; Assyria in a larger Persian Empire. In the Nile Valley small tribal communities are united into one kingdom, which falls apart, is re-united, and at last absorbed in more extended political structures. For two thousand years a Cretan civilization flourishes in the Aegean countries; it is suddenly half destroyed, half appropriated by the Greeks; the disunited Greek states, together with Egypt and the Persian Empire, are temporarily united by Alexander the Great, only to fall apart and be absorbed in the Mediterranean empire created by the Romans; the western half of the Roman Empire collapses under the impact of the German tribes, and on its ruins there arise many states and the unified structure of the Roman Church. Meantime, relatively large states contend for supremacy in India, while in China many contending states are finally united in one empire. In all this we note a marked acceleration in man's capacity to change his ways of living: the conflict and instability of his political structures is no less striking than their extension and power. We see the swift movement of hordes of men, the ceaseless march of disciplined legions; we hear the persistent and furious clash of arms, the triumphant cries of conquering hosts, the despairing lamentation of entire peoples carried off to slave in strange lands or left helpless amidst the ruins of their devastated cities.

The creation of these extended political structures, composed of many peoples of diverse custom and tradition, is accompanied by a striking modification of social organization. We note at once that the primitive tribal group is differentiated into fixed classes performing specialized functions. Look where we will there is essentially the same social hierarchy — slaves reduced to the status of beasts of burden; the mass of the people tilling the soil for a bare subsistence; dwellers in towns applying their skill to the mechanic and industrial arts; privileged landowners living on the toil of peasants; priests and scribes keeping the records, guarding the ritual, perpetuating and interpreting the tradition; civil and military officials making manifest the dignity and enforcing the power of the king; and the king himself, that "collective representative" of the most pervasive force (Totem, Moira, Gods) which is in and behind the world of men and things, whose will has now, even in defiance of custom long established, the force of law. The individual emerges from the undifferentiated tribal mass — a few individuals at the top; power is increased by being concentrated in them, and progress is effected by an enforced specialization of function in their interest. We note the progress that is made: progress in knowledge and reflection by the scribes who have leisure to keep and study the records; progress in the useful and the fine arts by craftsmen and artists who have no longer to hunt or till the soil for food; progress in luxurious living by the privileged who live on the unearned rent of land; progress in the structural arts by engineers and scientists who design temples in honor of the gods, or palaces and monuments to enhance the majesty of kings. In Sumeria and Babylonia, in Egypt and Crete and Greece, in China and India we see craftsmen and artists making useful objects of unsurpassed perfection. We see scribes and learned men copying and recopying records that accumulate in libraries, at Nineveh and Alexandria. We see, at Karnak and Athens, magnificent temples raised in honor of the gods; and splendid palaces — at Babylon, Nineveh, Cnossus — erected by royal order and paid for out of the spoils of conquered countries. We see engineers calculating with unprecedented precision the shape and stress of more than two million limestone blocks, of an average weight of more than two tons, to be fitted into the Great Pyramid, the most stupendous and enduring material monument ever constructed by men; and we see thousands of slaves and peasants toiling under the lash for twenty years

that the mummy of Khafra the Sun King may rest forever in peace.

That these creatures have transcended the narrow
static world of primitive experience is obvious; but
we may well ask whether it be not the Sword rather
than the Pen that has enabled them to do so. Nevertheless, if the Sword seems mightier than the Pen, that
is only because the Pen is less visible and noisy. Looking more attentively at what lies beneath the outward
activities of men, we see that the Sword and the Pen
work together — a striking confirmation of Bacon's
saying that human knowledge and human power
meet in one: without the Pen, the Sword could never
have become so much heavier than it was; without the
Sword, the Pen would never have had much to do except to keep accounts and chronicle small beer. The
states and empires displayed before us are conquered
or defended or destroyed by force of arms, but without written records they cannot be long sustained.
Wherever there appears an extended social structure,
together with the military power to guarantee it,
there emerge the individual leader (Prince, King,
Imperator) who gives orders, agents who receive and
execute the orders, subjects who are disciplined in the
habit of changing their habits, of departing from customary ways long established, in conformity with the

orders given. That orders may be relevant to the situation, the leader and his agents and his subjects must know much that they cannot know directly — must know and see imaginatively much that lies beyond the range of personal experience. Oral tradition is no longer sufficient; the written record, the signed and sealed and swiftly transmitted dispatch is essential. And we can in fact see the king's messengers, in relays, hastening along the king's highway from Susa to Sardis, from Rome to far-off Gaul and Britain, carrying the indispensable clay tablet or papyrus or parchment record that conveys, to civil and military officials alike, the will of the Prince. The extended social structure is held together, if at all, by the multiplication of written records which alone enable dispersed communities to hold in mind, superimposed upon the consciousness of custom instinctively followed, a common ideal image of words spoken, events occurring, enterprises initiated and carried through in times and places beyond the range of personal experience.

### 3

It is thus clear that man has made notable progress during the Third Period by virtue of having at his disposal mental and physical powers unknown to primitive men. We note, however, that these powers are not exerted, this progress is not shared, by all. The progress which accompanies the extension of man's power is purchased at a price: the price is the emergence of the individual, the exaltation of the few at the expense of the many. Within the extended political structure, the power of the community is exerted only by being concentrated in the exalted individual, the superior class, to whose will the mass of the people is subordinated by royal decrees that at once modify and reinforce custom. We thus look in vain for the social solidarity, the psychological uniformity, of the primitive community. What we see is differentiation, the multiplication of distinctions, a greater complexity, an increased instability. The social solidarity of the primitive community gives way to differentiated classes with specialized functions and graded rights and duties; the dead level of its psychological uniformity, disrupted by the graduation of classes, is replaced by different levels of intellectual apprehension. The mass of the people, since they are the instruments rather than the possessors of the new powers, rise but little and slowly above the level of primitive experience. Artisans and mechanics, occupied with the task of shaping material things, become the corporate guardians and transmitters of their arts and mysteries — the durable matter-of-fact knowledge

54

that arises from the manipulation of tools and implements. Superior to these are the priests and scribes, whose function it is to interpret the slowly changing tradition and thereby provide an ideal justification for established authority. This function they always and everywhere perform; but the magic of the written record is an implement of power more dangerous than they know: certain superior individuals, applying their minds to the written records, to the symbols of things rather than to the things themselves, are imperceptibly, even unconsciously, enticed beyond the known world of concrete experience into the uncharted realm of conceptual relations.

The realm of conceptual relations can be created only within an enlarged Time and Space universe. We can observe, although not too clearly, the persistent effort of men to extend the time world, to make vivid and precise the sense of time passing and passed. The rising sun separates today from yesterday, the inconstant moon differentiates the passing days into manageable groups. In Egypt, where life depends upon the good behavior of the Nile, men observe that the annual overflow comes (very nearly) at the time when the sun and the star Sirius appear together on the horizon: the calendar is thus invented, the time-scale of the year made precise — twelve moons of thirty days each, with five days left over for feasting. Yet the years pass, and, as they recede, they melt into undifferentiated Time-Passed, except for certain years that are identified by striking events not easily forgotten. The Sumerians do not forget the year when the world was nearly destroyed by the Great Flood, which becomes for them a point in time dividing the years before from the years after. Not every people has experienced so memorable an event; but other people have their kings, those deified personifications of power, who do not permit themselves to be easily forgotten; and we can see men making lists of their kings and the number of years each one has reigned, so that Time-Passed comes to be visualized as a series of receding dynasties. Yet time is long and life is short. Time stretches back to the beginning of things, and the list of known kings will not reach so far unless the first kings lived longer than now. It must have been so in that far-off time: kings, being then greater, must have lived longer. The Chinese know that in the beginning were the thirteen Celestial Emperors, each of whom reigned eighteen thousand years. The Sumerians can read the list of sixty kings who ruled during the 31,076 years after the Great Flood, and the list of eight kings who ruled during the 241,000 years before the Great Flood. Thus Time-Passed, filled in by the visual image of the heroic long-lived kings, is pushed back to the beginning of the world, to the Garden of Eden, to the Golden Age of King Chronos, or the era of Pan-Ku, creator of the universe.

As the Time world is ideally extended beyond the range of remembered things, so the Space world is ideally extended beyond the range of known places. To the early Sumerians "the world" seems no more than the valley they inhabit, something that malicious gods can destroy by an inundation of the Two Rivers. Centuries pass, and the world is larger, yet not so large but that kings of Sumer and Akkad, pushing their conquests to the Mediterranean, are celebrated as rulers of "the four regions of the earth" from the "rising to the setting sun." Other centuries pass, and Thutmose III proclaims himself "lord of the world." Yet "lord of the world" is now no more than a pardonable royal boast, since it is known that there are other worlds to conquer. A thousand years later, King Xerxes is lord of a world that extends from the Indus to the Danube, but is well aware that there are regions yet unsubdued — upper Egypt, and India, and the Aegean Lands inhabited by the presumptuous Hellenes. The Hellenes themselves know that there is a sea beyond the Pillars of Hercules; the Father of History, insatiably inquiring about every strange thing, has heard of ships sailing the southern seas to Far Eastern countries; and Eratosthenes (200 B.C.) can make a foreshortened, streamlined map of the known and heard-of countries of the earth that extends from Ceylon to Britannia, Ierne (Ireland), and Ultima Thule (Iceland). Yet to Eratosthenes the earth is more than its known or heard-of regions, and the universe is more than the earth. In defiance of common sense he thinks of the earth as a sphere in the heavens among other spheres — the sun and the moon, and the stars whose names are given in the writings of Hipparchus. For four thousand years the universe has been expanding, if not in itself then in the mind of man; and as it expands it becomes differentiated — places known are distinguished from places heard of, places known and heard of are distinguished from places necessarily existing. The earth on which men live is both larger and smaller than it was: larger than the Valley of the Two Rivers, smaller than the comprehended universe of the heavenly bodies.

Within this enlarged Time and Space world not all that is apprehended is concrete, not all that is known is known with equal certainty. Since the image of such a world can be held together only by the nexus of the general concept, the idea of things is differentiated from the things themselves, and there is disclosed to men's view a fatal dualism — diverse and conflicting phenomena which, distressing the heart and perplexing the mind, call for appraisal and reconciliation. It is obvious that the slave is more oppressed than the peasant, the peasant more oppressed than the artisan; that the artisan is less privileged than the noble, the noble less godlike than the king. Learned men know that the event remembered is different from the event recorded, that the custom that once was is superseded by the custom that now prevails, the custom that now prevails by the law to be presently imposed. All who suffer and reflect are aware that individual purpose is frustrated by desire and thwarted by social compulsion, and that the utmost endeavors of men cannot always prevail against the implacable force of Nature. These perplexing contrasts raise questions, questions engender doubt. It seems that the outer world of things is after all not an integral and harmonious extension of man's personality. Gradually, imperceptibly, there emerges the most devastating of all facts: Man, who alone knows and aspires, lives but a brief moment in an indifferent universe that alone endures.

> *The generations pass away,*
> *While others remain . . . .*
> *None cometh from thence . . . .*

## Progress and Power

*That he may tell us of their fortunes,*
*That he may content our heart,*
*Until we too depart*
*To the place where they have gone.*

Faced by the fatal dualism disclosed within an ideally
extended realm of experience, superior minds turn
away from the effort to master the outer world of
means and quantity, in order to understand the inner
world of ends and quality. Distressed by the frailty
and impermanence of man's endeavors, they ask the
fundamental questions. What is the origin and end of
life? What is the meaning of existence? Why is it that
men, in an endless succession of passing generations,
live to know, struggle to attain, and attain, and attain
only to be defeated in the end?

The sense of utter defeat being intolerable, man is
not easily defeated, and answers to these questions are
therefore found. Differing superficially, and on different levels of apprehension, the answers are fundamen-
tally much the same: it is the body of man that dies,
his spirit survives; it is in appearance only that the
outward world of things is indifferent, behind appearance there is a universal essence (Brahma, Tao,
Moira, Fate, God, Absolute Idea, Right Reason, Natural Law) that is intelligent and purposeful, that is

at least reliable and not unfriendly. Between the spirit of man and the universal essence there is no ir- reconcilable disharmony: the spirit of man suffers af- fliction here and now, and suffering affliction it seeks permanence — the perfection that is not here and now but elsewhere and othertime, above or beyond or outside all that is transient and incomplete; it seeks the Way, the Word, the Truth that will lead it out, set it free, bring it into harmony with the universal essence that is and will forever remain good. Man is not easily defeated; over death itself he wins an ideal victory: finding that within the world of concrete ex- perience things are not an integral and harmonious extension of himself, he creates a realm of conceptual experience in which the idea of things is a projection of the Absolute Idea, and the spirit of man an integral and harmonious extension of the universal spirit.

Not to master the external world of things, but to reconcile the individual with the universal spirit be- comes then the supreme object of life. Within a brief span of centuries there appear, almost contemporane- ously, certain superior individuals (Buddha and Lao- Tsze and Confucius, Solomon and Job and Zoroaster, Socrates and Plato and Aristotle), philosophers and sages and prophets more powerful than kings, who teach men the way to transcend the frustrations and inequities of life, the appointed ways of circumventing death — death of the body and disillusionment of the spirit. There is the way of renunciation, of withdrawal from the evil world of things — liberating the spirit by crucifying the flesh. There is the way of fortitude in well doing — "not to act from personal motive, to conduct affairs without feeling the trouble of them, to account the great small and the small great, to recompense injury with kindness." There is the way of moderation and the golden mean — "Do not do to others what you would not have them do to you" — "Recompense kindness with kindness, but recompense injury with justice." There is the way of good works — relieving the distressed, giving to the poor, rendering unto Caesar the things that are Caesar's and unto God the things that are God's. There is the way of understanding — fortifying the mind by intellectual participation in the universal Right Reason, stoically adjusting the conduct to implacable Fate or the compulsion of Natural Law.

Following these appointed ways, the individual may now and here attain a measure of perfection in an imperfect world. But a part of the imperfect world is the social system of human relations; and the emergence of individuals who seek perfection within it discloses to view, for comparison and judgment, a fla-

grant difference between the social world as it is and
as it ought to be. Convinced that it ought to be better
than it is, men easily believe that it once was so: and
belief, confirmed by ancient records, leads to knowledge. It is thus known that the social world was better, was what it ought to be, what the universal spirit
meant it to be, in the beginning — in that far-off
heroic time depicted by the poets, the time of the
beneficent long-lived kings. Confucius knows that
since the ordered rule of the Celestial Emperors "the
world has fallen into decay and right principles have
disappeared." The Egyptians know that there was
once an age of righteousness, but that now "the land
is left to those who do iniquity." The Greeks lament
the passing of the Golden Age of King Chronos when
men lived like gods, free from toil and grief. The Hebrews look back to the just reign of King David, and
beyond it to that earlier time when man's first parents
dwelt in innocence in the Garden of Eden. In contrast to society as it is, there is thus disclosed an ideal
society created in the remote past by the gods or the
godlike kings, from which the present is a falling
away, a degeneration effected by fate or the fateful
gods as a consequence of human frailty, or as retribu-
tion for a disobedience of the spirit, a refusal to follow the appointed way.

## Progress and Power

The sense of having fallen away from an original
perfection destroys man's faith in unchanging tradition only to burden him with a sense of guilt and futility. His spirit is afflicted with pessimism, a nostalgia
for the lost youth of the world, so that perfection
seems attainable only by the superior individual, and
by him only through severe discipline. We see the cultivated Hindu withdrawing from the futility of practical activities to engage in the insecure refinements
of speculation, pursuing the endless weary journey of
the soul from incarnation to incarnation, sustained by
the somber hope that at some point in the eternal
passing his spirit may find the peace of Nirvana. We
see the Chinese making a virtue of resignation, seeking the quiescence recommended by Lao-Tsze, or en-
deavoring to avoid the displeasure of gods and ancestors by practicing the prudent maxims of Confucius.
We see the Egyptians, haunted by a sense of impermanence, laboring with the ingenuity of desperation
to preserve the perishable body in tombs designed to
resist the attrition of time itself. We see the Greeks
losing faith in the gods only to be confronted by an
inscrutable Moira, a blind implacable Fate, at best an
impersonal Law of Nature which decrees that men
and things alike are subject to the principle of eternal
recurrence, an endless repetition of the familiar phe-

nomena of growth and decay. Since perfection is
scarcely attainable for the few, what hope is there for
the many? For the many there is endurance, obedience to king and priest, at best the fearful prospect of
an uncertain existence in the dim underworld, the
shadow-life after death.

Nostalgia for the past deprives man of confidence
in the future. He feels insecure in a world that
changes, and helpless in one that changes only for the
worse. Unable himself to restore the Golden Age of
the past, he awaits the intervention of the gods or the
return of the godlike kings. In Greece, during the
brief moment while society is a small affair, men have
confidence, if not in the return of King Chronos, at
least in the appearance from time to time of the inspired legislator (Lycurgus, Solon, Cleisthenes) to set
things right, well aware that from this setting right
Fate or human frailty will effect another falling away
until another inspired legislator comes to set things
right again. After Cleisthenes, in the time of troubles,
we see Plato devising a constitution for Athens — a
republic in which philosopher-kings will always rule,
since "cities will not cease from ill" until philosophers
become kings or kings philosophers. Yet Plato is ig-
nored, the city-states are swept within the all-embrac-
ing Roman Empire, and when the philosopher-king,

Marcus Aurelius, appears at last, the task of regenerating the Roman Empire is too formidable: instead of setting things right, the philosopher-king communes with his own soul and counsels resignation. Since time is the enemy of man, the rational mind will cultivate the golden mean and steel itself to accept the blows of Fate with equanimity: without fear, but also without illusion, it will look into "the infinitude of time" and comprehend the "cyclical regeneration of all things" and discern that "our children will see nothing fresh, just as our fathers too never saw anything more than we," so that "the man of forty years, if he have a grain of sense, in view of this sameness has seen all that has been and shall be."

To deliver man from this endless sameness the return of the godlike king is not enough: the gods themselves must intervene. The Hebrews, having suffered more intolerable disasters than others, learn this truth. They too once looked forward to the return of the godlike king — a scion of the house of David. But they see their earthly kingdom destroyed and themselves dispersed in strange lands. Since there is no longer an earthly kingdom, it cannot be an earthly king that will come, but the Messiah foretold by the prophets, a spiritual king who will set things right in an ideal kingdom of Israel. Presently the man Jesus appears, teaching the equality of all men, doing good works, performing miracles, dying on the cross. Obscure disciples tell the story of his life and works, his death and resurrection; and throughout the harsh Roman world the poor and oppressed receive the glad tidings: the Messiah has appeared, has delivered God's promise that he will come again in glory to judge the world, separating good and evil men. In that last day all earthly kingdoms will end, the earth itself will be swallowed up in flames, and all the faithful will be gathered together with God in the Heavenly City, there to dwell in perfection forever. The endless circle is broken: God himself has intervened to reveal the meaning of life and to invest it with dramatic significance. In the beginning was the ideal society; the present is evil, but it is a temporary probation only, a time of testing; in the end the ideal society will be restored and perpetuated for the righteous. The Golden Age of the past is thus projected into the future, and perfection, so far from being something to look back upon with regret, becomes something to look forward to with hope — God's promised reward which the many as well as the few may win by right living.

In these varied ways, within the Third Period on our Time-Scale, men endeavor to circumvent death —

death of the body and disillusionment of the soul: oppressed by the impermanence and futility of man's endeavors, superior individuals for the most part turn away from the effort to master the outer world of things in order to attain, with the aid of whatever gods there be, spiritual perfection in an ideal realm of conceptual relations. Nevertheless, the effort to master the outer world of things is not abandoned. We see everywhere obscure artisans and artists, mechanics and engineers, improving their tools and implements of power, training the eye and the hand to a defter practice and the mind to a more acute understanding of their arts, and thereby accumulating and transmitting from generation to generation an ever increasing and more precisely ordered body of matter-of-fact knowledge of the form and pressure and behavior of material objects. We also see, here and there, a few eccentric individuals (Pythagoras, Eratosthenes, Euclid, Archimedes) exploring the most rarefied regions within the realm of conceptual relations, and thereby discovering the science of mathematics, which disclose to their view a fact as fascinating as it is useful — the fact that there is a precisely measurable relation between the behavior of concrete material objects and their unsubstantial ideal forms. We hear Pythagoras declaring the strange doctrine that number is the source of all things. We see Eratosthenes measuring the shadow cast by the sun in order to determine the circumference of the earth, and Archimedes looking for a fulcrum strong enough to sustain the lever with which to move it. These eccentric individuals have discovered a secret of profound import — a secret which gives them command of the one intellectual tool capable of effecting the reconciliation, which philosophers seek for in vain, between the world as disclosed to the senses and the world as disclosed to Right and Reason.

The secret known to the Greek mathematicians dies with them. It matters but little, since the secret can be of little further use until a later time — the time of da Vinci and Galileo, of Newton and Einstein — when new sources of power and more precise instruments for measuring and exerting it are available. Once possessed of these new sources of power and instruments of precision, men will turn with enthusiasm to the problem that so largely occupied primitive men, the problem of mastering the outer world of things; while a notable success in solving this problem will enable them to accept, if not precisely the primitive belief, at least the primitive belief in reverse form, the belief that man's personality is an integral and harmonious extension of that outer world of things. In the measure that this belief appears tenable, they will lose interest in the ultimate reconciliation of the individual soul with the universal essence, and, dispensing with the assistance of the gods, rely upon themselves to find the appointed way of salvation by subduing the impersonal forces of nature to the service of immediate and mundane human purposes.

# III

# Instruments of Precision

$dS/dt$ is always positive

## 1

WE HAVE NOW surveyed briefly the course of human history during the first three periods along a Time-Scale of 506,000 years, in the effort to discover a correlation between the extension of man's activities and the expansion of his intelligence, on the one hand, and the implements of power at his disposal, on the other. There remains for examination the Fourth Period — a scant thousand years from the discovery of magnetic force to the present time.

The discovery of magnetic force is of slight significance in itself. Its significance is in what it points to: it is a premonitory indication of the outstanding characteristics of the period that lies before us. A hasty glance at the Fourth Period as a whole enables us to see what those characteristics are: the discovery of new sources of power of unprecedented efficacy, the invention of instruments of precision for measuring and exerting the power available, and an ever more deliberate and systematic effort to master the outer world of nature and to subdue it to human use. It is by these characteristics alone that we can clearly distinguish the Fourth Period from the Third. If we were observing human activity from the forum or the market place, the distinction would be obscured by a multiplicity of ephemeral events; but from remote Olympus the rise and fall of empires appear less striking than the fact that for five thousand years few if any new sources of power were discovered, and that as a consequence the implements of power at man's disposal at the end of that time, although far more numerous and more efficiently elaborated, were in kind essentially the same as at the beginning. We note then that there are two chief periods of power-implement discovery — the second and the fourth. Very nearly all of the sources and implements of power essential to community living were discovered by primitive men; all others, or very nearly all, make their appearance during the last thousand years on the Time-Scale. In this sense the Third Period discloses itself to our view as an interlude — the time when man's most notable efforts were devoted to exhausting the possibilities presented by the invention of writing, doing what could be done with the aid of the written record: creating more extended and elaborate social structures, exploring the realm of conceptual relations, habituating and disciplining the mind to such expertness in the manipulation of ideas as might be achieved by the use of verbal symbols. The possibilities of progress along this line of endeavor appear to have been exhausted early in the fourth millennium of the Third Period: thereafter, for more than a thousand years, nothing emerges in the way of philosophical speculation, of religious doctrine or ethical judgment, of aesthetic or mathematical competence, of legal or political theory, that could not have been easily grasped by Buddha or Lao-Tsze or Confucius, Socrates or Plato or Aristotle, the Stoic philosophers or the Roman jurisconsults. Nevertheless, the interlude lingers on, in some places longer than in others — in China and India, for example, until the present time.

The first to emerge from the interlude of the Third Period are the Europeans. They alone initiate the Fourth Period by gradually losing interest in the manipulation of ideas through the medium of verbal symbols and becoming increasingly absorbed in the manipulation of things with the aid of mathematical concepts. This shift of interest is at first accomplished slowly, and for the most part unconsciously; but during the last three centuries it becomes at once more rapid, more deliberate, and more complete. It is during these three centuries that the Europeans (with whom the Americans are to be included) discover in quick succession the chief new sources of power (steam, electricity, radiation), invent the instruments of precision appropriate to them, and turn with conscious purpose and systematic deliberation to the task of subduing the outer world of nature to human use. To the accomplishment of this task other peoples contribute almost nothing, so that the Fourth Period appears to exist for Europeans and Americans alone: other people share in it, so to speak, only vicariously.

Yet this is appearance merely — an illusion engendered by the abrupt termination of the Time-Scale, which induces us to see the Fourth Period as already completed. The Fourth Period, it is safe to assume, is no more than well begun, and in order to see it properly we need to project it, imaginatively into the future. It is properly represented on the Time-Scale as 1,000 $x$ years, $x$ being an unknown number of years to come. What value may we safely give to $x$? Let us suppose that $x$ is five hundred years. Even allowing for the acceleration of man's capacity to shift his interest, it is unlikely that within a less time men will either exhaust the possibilities of power discovery or grow

weary of the implements that give to their possessors
ascendancy over men and things. Power possessed will
be used, and those who have it not must either master
or be mastered by it. And in fact, at the very end of
the Time-Scale, we can see the Japanese eagerly ap-
propriating, for defense or aggression, the new implements of power, and the Chinese, more reluctantly,
preparing to follow their example. We may safely assume, therefore, that the Fourth Period will last at
least five hundred years longer, and that within that
brief time the Oriental peoples, even if only under
compulsion, will fully appropriate the science and
technology discovered by the Western world and acquire the mentality engendered by their use.

At this point a philosopher, if there be one left
among us, may well ask why the Europeans are the
first, and for nearly a thousand years the only ones, to
become sufficiently preoccupied with the outer world
of things to devise the implements of power essential
to its control. That question we cannot answer. But
since the Europeans are differentiated from others in
this respect, we will look for some other persistent activity that is likewise peculiar to them. We see at once
that there is another persisting activity: whereas other
peoples — the Hindus and the Chinese and the Hel-
lenized peoples of western Asia — remain relatively

immobile, fixed within the places where they have long dwelt, content with repeating the activities and adhering to the ideas that use and custom make familiar, the Europeans alone are always on the move, pushing beyond their frontiers, spreading themselves ever more dominantly over the habitable globe. This persistent enterprise is not accomplished without an increasing expertness in the realm of practical activities, still less without acquiring new ideas engendered by the stimulus of novel experience. There may then be a connection between the expansion of Europeans throughout the world, their preoccupation with practical activities, and their success in discovering the sources and implements of power that facilitate their mastery of the world of men and things. The connection will become clearer perhaps if we note more attentively the early stages in this double expansion of intelligence and power.

2

We begin then with the Europeans, at the opening of the Fourth Period, before they venture abroad. It seems at first unlikely that they will accomplish great things, since they appear to have forgotten much that was formerly known. The once ordered Roman Empire has given place to a multiplicity of petty principalities with little to unite them except a common faith and the unified structure of the Christian Church. The great majority of the people are serfs attached to the soil; there are few towns; the industrial and mechanic arts are of slight importance; commerce scarcely exists. Of the ruling class of nobles and priests, the former are untutored and warlike, the latter devoted to guarding the doctrine and administering the ritual of the Church. Nobles and priests alike live in a small world, having lost contact both with other peoples and with their own historic past. They know too little of ancient Greece and Rome to feel the loss of that vanished grandeur, nor does it distress them to recall the initial ideal state of man in the Garden of Eden, since they are well assured of felicity and perfection in the future Heaven reserved for believers in the one true God. Thus their very limitations of which they are unaware enable the Europeans, more than others, to escape pessimism, the sense of man's futility, nostalgia for the Golden Age. They are the chosen people; the others are heretics or Infidels whom it is a virtue to pity and a duty to despise. Armed with confidence born of ignorance and with arrogance engendered by dogmatic faith, they are well prepared to make the best of two worlds, alternately fighting each other for material advantage and uniting against the Infidels for the promotion of truth and righteousness.

Thus equipped, the Europeans set out on their conquest of the world. In the Christian year 1096 we see a band of Norman knights moving to the east, expelling the Infidels from the Holy City, and establishing there a European kingdom of Jerusalem. It is the First Crusade, so historians tell us, and they tell us that there were ten Crusades in the two centuries following. We will appropriate the word, but extend the time. From Olympus we can see that the Crusade goes on, with temporary reversals and intermissions, for a thousand years, is still going on: the Crusade goes on, assuming many forms, never quite lacking an ideal sanction, yet ever more subtly guided by practical material interests. For the Infidels are found to be richly supplied with desired things not obtainable in Europe, and we see the first Crusaders bringing back to their sparely furnished castles silks and tapestries, spices and strange dyes and precious stones — and gold. We see the ducat minted, and the florin and the gold coins of Louis IX. Presently the industrial arts begin to flourish, towns multiply, and merchant princes in Germany and Italy accumulate wealth and govern powerful cities.

Yet spices are costly, middlemen take the profit, and

gold flows always back to the East, even to the East beyond the Holy Land. The mysterious East, where treasure is and the spices grow, lays its spell upon the European imagination: so that presently we see Portuguese ships creeping around Africa, reaching India, reaching the spice islands; and Columbus, provided with a compass, turning his Spanish galleys to the west, thinking this the shortest route to the East but finding a new world blocking the way; and Magellan, sailing around this unwanted obstruction, reaching the real Indies at last, circumnavigating the globe. What do they seek, these Crusaders? Adventure, no doubt, freedom to "follow the strong bent of their spirits": yet something more. We hear Vasco da Gama announcing his mission to the Hindus: "We come in search of Christians and spices." We hear Columbus: "Gold is excellent, gold is treasure, and he who possesses it does whatever he wishes in this life, and succeeds in helping souls into Paradise." In no long time the European Crusaders, equipped with newly discovered and deadly firearms, are securely intrenched in the Old World and the New — the two Indies — and while missionaries go out to spread the true faith, silver plate and cotton and sugar from America, spices and fabrics and treasure from Asia flow regularly into Europe, raising prices, impoverishing nobles, enriching burghers, who buy and sell — and lend money to kings for equipping armies and consolidating their power.

The expansion of the European Crusaders throughout the world during five hundred years is not accomplished without disciplining the mind to a more exact attention to the practical activities, without an increasing preoccupation with the material values of which money is at once the measure and the symbol. We see wealth, accumulated from industries that thrive on commerce beyond the seas, flowing into the tills of shopkeepers and tradesmen, the coffers of kings, and the treasury of the Church. With money taken from the Church or supplied by burghers, ambitious kings equip armies to consolidate their position in Europe, and navies to maintain commercial establishments in Asia and America. In a succession of wars they contend for mastery on land and sea; and we note that, while prestige passes from those states that lose to those that win ascendancy in the two Indies, power within the great states passes imperceptibly from country to town, from land to capital, from nobles and priests to merchants and traders. Under the stimulus of trade and industry the mechanic arts are perfected: implements long known are elaborated and new ones invented to facilitate the making and transport of goods and the communication of information, to increase the efficiency of shipping and navigation and the art of war. Under the patronage of princes and popes the plastic and the structural arts flourish: palaces are erected to enhance the majesty of kings, and temples of intricate design and haunting beauty arise to manifest the authority of the Church. The Church takes its share of accumulated wealth, only to be subordinated by kings to the support of impoverished but docile nobles, and as it puts on an external splendor its priests become absorbed in secular activities and lose their hold on the imagination of men.

As we survey human history during the first five hundred years of our Fourth Period, it thus becomes clear that the Europeans, unlike other peoples, greatly extend their activities, modify their way of living, and shift their predominant interest. Starting out as defenders of the Christian faith, they gradually lose interest in the Holy City and look for more tangible utopias: compromising with the Infidels in return for their fabrics and treasure, they become increasingly preoccupied with the outer world of things and with the implements essential to the appropriation of its material advantages. The social manifestation of this preoccupation is the increase in numbers and in power of the burgher class, which imperceptibly, unconsciously, imposes its mental temper on the European mind.

We need then to note more attentively the activities, the occupation and the preoccupations of the burghers — the *bourgeoisie*. They are neither nobles nor peasants, still less priests. They are the compactly living town-dwellers — artisans and mechanics and engineers, shopkeepers and merchant traders and the clerks and accountants that do their bidding, soldiers and sailors, master mariners and cartographers, lawyers and judges and scriveners, town councillors, administrators serving the king, bailiffs and feudists employed by nobles to put their affairs in order, bankers and speculators and the manipulators of guilds and trading companies, internationally-minded families of great wealth, strategically located in many countries, who develop mines, finance petty princes and bankrupt kings, and administer for a profit the grant of papal indulgence. Their power is derived neither from birth nor from office but from money, that abstract and conveniently supple measure of the material value of all things. They are occupied with immediately practical affairs, with defined and determinable rights, with concrete things and their disposal and their calculable cash value. Their hands are trained to the expert manipulation of tools and implements, their minds are disciplined to the performance of routine duties, to an exact attention to what is substantial and measurable, to what is persistent and uniform in recurrence, to what is probable and credible because evident to the senses. They are the inheritors and beneficiaries of that body of durable matter-of-fact knowledge that has accumulated and been transmitted from primitive times. Ideal and allegorical meanings are irrelevant to their activities: their one indispensable symbol is numbered, the precise measure of the extension of things and events in space and time. Of space as a measure of aspiration, of time as a symbol of the seven virtues, they can make no use; for them time and space are independent but co-ordinated extensions to be identified by the clock and the foot rule. The burgher mind is subdued to what it works in: chiefly occupied with practical affairs and material values, it seeks to impose on the outer world of things and relations an ordered and measurable and predictable behavior.

The burgher's preoccupation with matter-of-fact knowledge and an ordered and predictable outer world does not extend beyond the range of his practical interests, and as such it is nothing new. On the contrary it is his most direct inheritance from primitive times. Turning for a moment to observe the activities of primitive man, we see him shaping his axe and planting his seeds; and we see that he relies not wholly in vain upon the outer world to verify his prediction that the axe will cut and the seeds grow. The extent of his matter-of-fact knowledge is indeed limited; but such knowledge, not needing to be unlearned, is durable, capable of being transmitted through the generations and ages with little change; with little change except that in the process of transmission it is cumulatively extended and co-ordinated; and as it is extended and co-ordinated the range of experience within which man can rely with matter-of-fact assurance upon the outer world is enlarged. We note certain obvious stages in the enlargement of this realm of the matter-of-fact. Primitive man relies with more matter-of-fact assurance upon his axe than upon his seeds, with more assurance upon his seeds than upon the fertility of the earth. The ancient Egyptian relies with more assurance than primitive man upon the fertility of the earth; he relies with assurance upon the sun and the moon to measure the procession of the seasons, but has no assurance that the spirit that moves the sun and the moon will not be offended by his own actions. The ancient Greeks rely with assurance upon the uniform behavior of the outer world of familiar things and of the distant heavenly bodies, but they stand frustrate and perplexed by the behavior of inscrutable Moira, the implacable Fate that confuses the reason and disappoints the hopes of men.

The Europeans whom we are observing have not as yet made any notable extension of the realm of matter-of-fact known to the Greeks, but they have certain advantages, of traditional faith and acquired experience, that will presently enable them to do so. Not the least of these advantages is that they do not lack assurance. They have long since transcended pessimism, the sense of man's futility, by substituting for an implacable Fate an implacable but just God who has revealed to them the origin, the dramatic course, and the ultimate good end of human existence. The Revelation accustoms them to an ordered and predictable world, a world governed by the law of God, and assures them that they are the chosen people for whom it was designed. Acquired experience, their success in exploring and mastering the world of men and things, meanwhile leaves them ill disposed to submit to a fate wholly predetermined by a power not themselves, and yet fortifies their conviction that they are the chosen people whose destiny is in their own keeping. They begin to see themselves as adventurers, explor-

ers, the curious ones who will try anything once, ingenious devisers of implements of power that effectively serve their purposes. The expansion of their
practical activities is becoming sufficiently accelerated
for them to be aware of it, and aware that it is their
own doing, since great events and notable discoveries
are not accomplished so slowly that the beginning is
forgotten by those who witness the end. All men
can see that the discovery of America and the circum-
navigation of the globe are the swift, dramatic per-
formances of individual men who bring great things
to pass by deliberate effort guided by conscious purpose. Those who reflect can see this, yet something
more: they can see that action validates conjecture,
that experience confirms theory. Of what avail then is
the dispute between Eratosthenes and Ptolemy, or
the Revelation as an authority for deciding it, since
Columbus and Magellan have demonstrated both by
observation and by experiment that the earth is
round?

In extending their activities throughout the world
the European crusaders thus discover something more
than the compass or gunpowder or the art of printing
by movable type, something more than the New
World of America. They are discovering a new, or recovering an old technique for arriving at truth: their

own activities are disclosing to them a fatal diver-
gence between the truth of Revelation and the truth
that emerges from observed and tested experience.
The challenge does not disconcert them. Still following their practical interest, they accept the verdict of
experience, and thereby extend the realm of matter-
of-fact to include the entire outer world of things and
the intangible forces that are in and behind appearance. For the revealed story of the life of man they
will substitute a verified account of the factual experience of men; for the implacable and intelligent God
they will substitute an impersonal, universal Law of
Nature which, not being capricious or past finding
out, can be relied upon with the same matter-of-fact
assurance with which common men rely upon the familiar world of daily use.

3

Surveying the activities of men during the last
three hundred years of the Time-Scale we can see that
this extension of the realm of matter-of-fact to include
the intangible forces that are in and behind appearance is the chief contribution of the Europeans to the
expansion of human power and intelligence. It is an
extension of the common man's matter-of-fact apprehension, but it is a generalized and abstract extension,

not well understood by common men, that can be effected only by exceptional individuals. We see them emerging, these exceptional individuals, a new class of learned men, differentiated from the official priests and scribes: humanists and historians — the mechanics of the intellectual realm, erudite accumulators of matter-of-fact knowledge of man's activities in a time sequence; natural philosophers — verifying and tabulating the observed recurrences in the behavior of material things; mathematicians, the high priests of the new science — rediscovering Archimedes' secret, noting with increasing refinement the relation between the behavior of material things and their unsubstantial idea forms. We note that these exceptional individuals "do not reply to their predecessors, they bid them goodby." They do not ask what is officially said to be true, or what tradition holds it reasonable to suppose must be so: observing what does in fact occur, what has in fact happened, they announce what as a matter of fact is true of this particular thing, of that particular event. We can see, what they could not, that they are dispensing with the assistance of the gods in the effort to find out for themselves what man has in fact done (History), how things do in fact behave (Science).

We see them emerging, these exceptional individuals: Copernicus and Kepler and Galileo, conveniently assuming that the earth and planets move around the sun, and thereby finding the calculations of their observed behavior much simplified. The assumption appears to "cover the facts" and is therefore taken for true: it need not declare the glory of God, since it lightens the burden of mathematicians. In this casual way the earth is displaced from the center of creation and takes its place as a minor planet, while man sees his stature diminish as the comprehended universe is infinitely expanded. The immense spaces affright him momentarily, but he reflects that "thought makes the dignity of man," and is not long disheartened by his apparent insignificance since he has himself discovered it: is encouraged rather, as he discovers that the universe of infinite spaces, insensitive to his fate though it may be, is amenable to his control. For there is Galileo, discovering the law of nature — measuring the accelerating velocity of falling bodies; and Newton, with the aid of the differential calculus, measuring the force of gravitation that holds the universe together. It is not the concept of natural law that they discover, but the law itself. The concept is old in tradition — is in Aristotle and the Stoics, the Jurisconsults and the Christian philosophers, who infer from the rational nature of God that Nature is not

recalcitrant to Right Reason. But Galileo and Newton do not infer that Nature is lawful because God is
rational; having transposed the verbal concept of natural law into mathematical formulae, they infer from
the measured mechanical behavior of Nature that
God is an engineer — the Great Contriver or Prime
Mover, who has so constructed the universe of immense spaces that it may be mastered by the hand as
well as contemplated by the spirit of man. In the law
of falling bodies, Archimedes, if he were with us,
would at once recognize the fulcrum for moving the
world which he sought in vain.

While natural philosophers are disclosing an ordered and predictable outer world that is amenable
to man's control, humanists and historians are disclosing a world of human activities that is ever changing,
yet not necessarily for the worse. There are the humanists (from Petrarch to Erasmus and Montaigne)
piously recovering and critically examining lost or
forgotten works of ancient writers; and the historians
(from Guicciardini to Montesquieu and Gibbon) fill-
ing in and making vivid the half-empty Time-Passed
with a matter-of-fact story of man's activities from remote beginnings. In the light of recorded history, the
revealed story of man's life and destiny fades away
into the realm of myth, and the initial ideal state of

man is transferred from the Garden of Eden to the Golden Age of Greek and Roman civilization. Dazzled by this brilliance, men for a moment distrust their own abilities and are afflicted with nostalgic regret for the vanished grandeur of the ancients. Yet only for a moment. The Dark or Middle Age intervening between them and the Romans is after all no more than a temporary decline and fall into barbarism and superstition, from which they see themselves rapidly emerging by virtue of having recovered all that the ancients knew. It occurs to them then that they themselves, the "moderns," are the true ancients, since they are the latest in the succession of generations, while the ancients whom they revere are the young, those who lived in the youth of the world. Surely the late-comers, having appropriated the knowledge and profited by the errors of past generations, should be able to surpass their predecessors; and, having surpassed them, transmit to future generations the accumulated experience which will enable their descendants to surpass the generations of men now living. They can therefore face the future with renewed confidence, revering their ancestors less as they think better of themselves and expect more of posterity.

Thus there emerges, within the European climate

of opinion, and as a rationalization of the practical interests of a burgher society, the idea of human Progress. During five hundred years the adventurous Europeans have gradually pushed back the obscuring walls of the spatial and temporal universe until, by an imaginative flight from the here and now, man can see himself functioning within an ordered and predictable outer world that may be controlled, and within a developing social world that changes for the better with the increase and refinement of knowledge. Within this expanded Time and Space frame of reference, man and Nature appear once more in harmonious relation, since Nature is designed according to unvarying laws that reveal its meaning, and man is endowed with an intelligence capable of discovering that meaning for himself. There is then no need for a special revelation, since God has spoken to men through the articulated mechanism of Nature. We hear the pregnant question: "Is it natural, is it reasonable that God should go in search of Moses in order to speak to Jean Jacques Rousseau!" Man has only to read the open Book of Nature to learn the meaning of existence and to adjust his way of life to cosmic intention. The long-treasured vision of a Golden Age, once identified with the creation of the world by capricious, inscrutable gods, and then trans-

92

ferred to the beatific life after death in the Heavenly City, is at last identified with the progressive amelioration of man's earthly state by the application of his intelligence to the mastery of the outer world of things and to the conscious and rational direction of social activities.

In following the slowly accelerating expansion of human power and intelligence along a Time-Scale of 506,000 years, we thus arrive at the point where progress and the idea of progress are conjoined. We feel that the event should prove to be a notable one, and we are curious to see what will come of it. But time is running short, a scant three hundred years remaining on our Time-Scale; and we may think it unlikely that anything new and strange can occur in that brief moment of human history. Nevertheless, we need not despair of man's capacity to upset our expectations. Of all the inventions yet made by the ingenious Europeans, the doctrine of progress is the most effective, the most revolutionary and dislocating, since it transforms a Deo-Centric into a Homo-Centric universe, and thereby makes man the measure of all things. By liberating the mind from fear of the gods and the restraints of tradition, it invites men to pursue without inhibitions the call of their desires; while by locating perfection in the future and identifying it with the successive achievements of mankind, it makes a virtue of novelty and disposes men to welcome change as in itself a sufficient validation of their activities. If then the idea of progress emerges from progress itself, progress is in turn reinforced by the idea of progress that is in men's minds. Which is cause, which effect, we need not inquire: we note merely that during the brief three hundred years remaining on our Time-Scale there occurs an unanticipated and quite unprecedented expansion of human power and intelligence, a quite unprecedented acceleration of man's capacity to control the outer world of things and to modify his traditional ideas and social habits.

The beginning of this brief but momentous three hundred years we will place at the moment when Newton is formulating the universal law of gravitation, which is the moment when Newcomen is trying to devise a workable steam engine, the moment also when the idea of progress is disclosing to men the hope of a resplendent future. We note that, in the century following, men become increasingly conscious of living in an age of Enlightenment, of Clarification: common sense reason, and matter-of-fact knowledge, washed clear of enthusiasm and illusion, are exposing old errors and superstitions, justifying the ways of Nature to men's desires, disclosing the capacity of the natural man for moral and social perfection. Never did the universe appear less mysterious or more easily manageable; never did man appear more simple, more pliable to the persuasive influence of rational instruction. The answers to all of man's unanswered questions, the solution of all of his unsolved enigmas appear to be at hand: he has but to adjust himself to the laws of Nature and of Nature's God, which are also the laws of his own being. We hear Condorcet announcing the fact, "The perfectibility of man is really infinite." It is in this optimistic age of common sense that we see men becoming conscious revolutionists, with systematic deliberation turning their minds to the discovery of Nature's secret laws and to the regeneration of social institutions.

Observing the course of this revolutionary attack, we note that the optimism of those who rely upon unvarying natural law to give them control over the outer world of things is justified beyond all expectation. An ever increasing number of exceptional individuals, inspired by the success and guided by the method of Galileo and Newton, devote themselves with impersonal curiosity to the exploration of the physical world, and thereby rapidly create the systematic and co-ordinated body of matter-of-fact knowledge that takes the name of natural science. The expansive force of steam, long known, is made available by the laws of mechanics, and new sources of power (electricity and radiation) are discovered, reduced to measured control, and applied to practical use. The discovery of new sources of power calls for the invention of new implements of precision for measuring and exerting the power available; while the multiplication of machines, machine tools, and appliances that serve the practical activities reinforces the systematic pursuit of scientific knowledge by enlisting the interest and support of the dominant burgher class. Thus science serves industry, industry endows science, and both the pursuit of knowledge and of profits calls for an ever increasing class of engineers, technicians, statisticians, and mechanics whose minds are disciplined to the matter-of-fact apprehension and stored with the matter-of-fact knowledge of things that alone make the new power available.

Under the impact of this deliberate and concerted attack upon the secrets of Nature, the slow-paced routine of man's activities is accelerated and loses its familiar pattern. The new power discovered by scientists and mediated by engineers is applied to all the diverse activities of men, but its most notable manifestations are in the realm of the mechanic and industrial arts. Within this realm the function of the new power is to accelerate the movement of men and things and thereby increase work done in relation to the time and the man-power required to do it. Speed and power become the symbols, quantity and precision the measure of achievement: speed and power in the mass-production of things desired, in the mass-movement of men and things from place to place; precision in the intermeshing relation of men and things in a pattern that becomes ever more extended and intricate as technical improvements overcome inertia and diminish the obstacles of time and space. Observing this process, we note an unprecedented acceleration in man's capacity to create material wealth; we note also that as instruments of power and precision multiply and are improved, the man-power required to create wealth declines. Men are themselves aware of these significant facts, and they look forward to the moment when, with slight effort on their part, instruments of power and precision will supply all that is needed: the moment when common men, hitherto condemned to live by unremitting labor, will have leisure for the pursuit of immaterial values, and can live — as in the mythical reign of King Chronos men lived — like the gods, free from toil and grief.

Nevertheless, from generation to generation the happy moment recedes, and the hopes of men are disappointed. The reason for this will perhaps appear if we contrast the revolution in scientific knowledge with the social revolution that runs parallel to it. To the philosophers of the century of Enlightenment the regeneration of society seems no different in character, and even less difficult to effect, than the exploitation of Nature's secrets: no different in character, since common-sense reason will disclose, in men as in things, the unvarying laws of Nature which God has imprinted on men and things alike; even less difficult to effect, since men, unlike things, will consciously co-operate in the adjustment of their social activities to these unvarying laws. "The constitution," we hear them announcing, "is already made since its eternal principles are engraved on the hearts of all men." This optimistic view is not justified in the events. It turns out that men are less tolerant of projects interesting to social reformers than things are of theories interesting to natural scientists. Unlike things, men are not indifferent to experiments made upon them, while those who carry through social revolutions do so, not with an impersonal matter-of-fact apprehension, but with an apprehension attentive to their own advantage. The social revolution is not carried through by philosophers standing apart from the men who are to be regenerated, but by the men themselves; and so it happens that the eternal laws of Nature, which philosophers think God has engraved on the hearts of all men, are hardly distinguishable from the ideas imprinted upon the minds of the dominant social class.

We note then that the dominant social class, the bourgeoisie, finding its expanding activities hampered by the arbitrary power of kings and the privileges of nobles and priests, identify the eternal law of Nature with the freedom of the individual from royal and corporate and class restraints. Philosophers tell them that when everyone is free all will be equal, when all are equal everyone will have enough, when everyone has enough no one will be unreasonable or inhumane. During a hundred years the social revolution follows this path, inspired by this hope. Kings are deposed in favor of representatives chosen by the people; the individual is emancipated from the class status, relatively stable, that from time immemorial defined his rights, prescribed his occupation, and bound him to long-established habits and ideas. Nevertheless, a society of equal, and equally rational and humane individuals does not emerge. Within an industrial society of uprooted and freely competing individuals, in which wealth replaces birth and occupation as the measure of power and prestige, there emerge certain individuals, favored above others by intelligence and opportunity, who acquire control of the new implements of power, appropriate the surplus wealth created by them, and purchase the services of the many in a labor market where the demand for man-power declines as the efficiency of machine-power increases. Thus the new power discovered by scientists and mediated by engineers is placed at the disposal of the few, and employed by them in a competitive struggle to maintain and extend their private advantage.

As the social revolution discloses this harsh fact, philosophers cease to predict the infinite perfectibility of man, but still declare that the unvarying law of Nature sanctions individual freedom in the economic realm, since the private profit of the few is obviously a public benefit. This view serves for a time — so long as the many are not too distressed, so long as the brilliant success of scientific knowledge applied to the production of wealth obscures the ominous fact that its proper distribution is left to chance, to the uncertain operation of individual self-interest. Yet from decade to decade the public benefit of this discordant system becomes less apparent as the ruthless competition for private profit leads to disastrous class conflict within, and to still more disastrous war between the nations: so little apparent that philosophers, unable any longer to distinguish right and force, identify the law of Nature with the unconscious will of man, and progress with an unremitting struggle for existence and survival. We thus note that during a hundred years the expansion of human intelligence and power discloses a significant contrast: while man's effort to control the forces of Nature is accompanied by increasing success and mounting optimism, his efforts to regenerate society lead only to confusion and despair.

This significant contrast is reflected in the activities of men as we observe them at the very end of our Time-Scale. We see no lack of fertile farms, of elaborate and fully equipped factories, no lack of engineers and technicians and mechanics to operate the factories and cultivate the farms, no lack of inventors with new devices for making machine-power more automatic and man-power less necessary. Yet we note that the factories are running intermittently or not at all, that the farms are cultivated only in part. It is not that all have enough; for we see millions of men and women, lacking the necessities of life, standing before the machines, competent and eager to operate them; and yet, like the machines themselves, standing idle and unsupplied. We see this, and something more: while millions of men stand idle before idle machines, other men in obedience to governmental decree, refrain from planting wheat and plow growing cotton under ground. A survey of human history will often enough disclose millions of men starving in time of famine: what we see now is something unprecedented — millions of men destitute in the midst of potential abundance. For there are the necessary instruments of precision, there are the engineers and technicians and mechanics with the necessary power and knowledge conjoined, ready and eager to supply men with all that they need, with much that they desire besides; yet there they stand, waiting as it were, while the people engage in furious class struggle and governments prepare for war and revolution.

> *Blight — not on the grain!*
> *Drouth — not in the springs!*
> *Rot — not from the rain!*
>
> *What shadow hidden or*
> *Unseen hand in our midst*
> *Ceaselessly touches our faces?* *

There is clearly some failure in co-ordinating the expanding activities of men, some radical discord between man's capacity to control the forces of Nature

* Archibald MacLeish, *Panic* (Boston, 1935), p. 8.

and his capacity to subdue his social relations to rational direction.

Since it is in the realm of material interests that this discord creates the most immediate and pressing distress, it is with the solution of economic problems that men are for the time being almost wholly occupied. The great majority, knowing that something is amiss, accept diverse explanations and welcome diverse remedies. There are those who maintain that all will be well if nothing is done, others who insist that unless something be done quickly still greater evils will befall. Among the latter are those who maintain that in the long run there can be neither private nor public advantage in employing the automatic machine to make things to sell for private profit, since the automatic machine can neither buy the things it makes nor, in the absence of man-power and wages, distribute them to an idle population. They therefore insist that the matter-of-fact knowledge so successfully applied to the making and transportation of things must be likewise applied to their proper social distribution. Everywhere men are discussing the "socialization of the means of production," the necessity of a "regulated economy," a "planned society." And in many countries those in authority are even attempting to apply these ideas in practice, inexpertly as we can see, still relying upon the intelligent response of common men to the available matter-of-fact knowledge, or turning to revolution and the direction of supermen, to effect an equitable distribution of wealth as the essential condition for establishing the long-dreamed-of society of equal and equally rational and humane individuals.

The effort is natural, even necessary, the inexpertness inevitable under the circumstances. For to us, taking a long-time view of human history, the economic disturbance that so aggravates passions and darkens counsel appears to be the surface symptom of a more profound social dislocation occasioned by the fact that mankind has entered a new phase of human progress — a time in which the acquisition of new implements of power too swiftly outruns the necessary adjustment of habits and ideas to the novel conditions created by their use. Long ago it was said that man can more easily take a city than govern himself; yet never before have men made relatively greater progress in the rational control of physical force, or relatively less in the rational control of social relations. The fundamental reason for this discrepancy is clear: it is that the forces of Nature have been discovered and applied by a few exceptional individuals, whereas every effort to ameliorate human relations has been frustrated by the fact that society cannot be transformed without the compliance of the untutored masses. The physical world of things, ignorant of and therefore undiverted by what men learn about it, can be relied upon to behave always in the same manner, and being indifferent to its own fate submits indifferently to whatever use men may wish to make of it. But the social world of men is neither unaware of nor indifferent to proposed modifications of its habitual behavior. It is therefore not enough that a few exceptional individuals should have discovered the advantages to be derived from rational social arrangements; in addition the masses who compose society must be persuaded or compelled to adapt their activities to the proposed changes, and the means of persuasion or compulsion must be suited to the apprehension of common men. The result is that those who have, or might acquire, the necessary matter-of-fact knowledge for adjusting social arrangements to the conditions created by technological progress have not the necessary authority, while those who have the necessary authority (representatives elected by the people, or dictators who act with their assent) must accommodate their measures to a mass intelligence that functions most effectively at the level of primitive fears and tabus.

105

Diverse and discordant views of the world and the life of man (all the levels of apprehension that have emerged since primitive times) present but not guaranteed in a society that has been so quickly and so profoundly transformed in its external aspects by matter-of-fact scientific knowledge — this, we can see, is the chief reason for man's failure to adjust his social activities to the expansion of his intelligence and power. The intelligence and power available cannot be fully employed, since it is the prerogative of the few, unshared because not understood by the many. This situation is indeed nothing new in itself, but only in the accentuation of its character and the flagrance of its disturbing effects. Ever since the psychological uniformity of primitive society gave way to different levels of apprehension, there has been a certain discrepancy between the sophisticated and the unsophisticated view of the world and the life of man; but until recently the chief function of the sophisticated, the priests and scribes, has been to stabilize custom and validate social authority by perpetuating the tradition and interpreting it in a manner conformable to the understanding of common men. During the last three hundred years this functional connection between the sophisticated and the unsophisticated has been broken, since there has emerged a new class of learned men, successors to the priests and scribes, whose function is to increase rather than to preserve knowledge, to undermine rather than to stabilize custom and social authority. Technological appliances and the symbols of fluid wealth that make precarious all material values have thus replaced a common faith in doctrines authoritatively taught as the chief means of social integration. The exceptional few have little in common with the undistinguished many, except the implements of power and the symbols of wealth with which to obtain them; so that while the outward activities of both are conditioned by the same material needs and appliances, their respective views of the world in which they both perforce live are too discordant to be easily woven into a harmonious pattern of psychological responses.

The exceptional few move with assurance and live at ease in an infinitely expanded time-and-space world. The matter-of-fact knowledge which enables them to supply common men with new and exciting implements of power enables them also to dispense with traditional views of the origin, the character, and the destiny of man. For them it is possible without distress to contemplate man as a biological organism that has slowly, through countless ages, emerged without credentials or instructions from a universe that is

as unaware of him as of itself and as indifferent to his
fate as to its own; for them it is possible without
strain to adjust their ethical judgments and social habits to the pragmatic implications of this enlarged time-
and-space frame of reference. But within this enlarged
frame of reference common men are not at home. No
longer sustained by traditional doctrines authoritatively taught, and yet incapable by themselves of applying the scientific apprehension to the problems
presented by a society so complex and so unstable,
they wander aimless and distrait in a shadowy realm
of understanding, alternately enticed by venerable
faiths that are suspect but not wholly renounced and
by the novel implications of factual knowledge accepted on rumor but not understood. Swayed by passions engendered by economic distress, the common
man is thus the more easily persuaded by leaders who,
intent upon their own advantage or impelled by a
genuine sense of duty, follow the line of least intelligence in order to provide the masses with such ideas
only as are palatable to them, such ideas only as are
easily sustained by the profound satisfaction that
comes from imitative action. Truth emerges from an
agreement of minds, and for common men minds
agree most effectively when bodies act in unison. Myr-
iad hands lifted in salute are more convincing than

facts or syllogisms, whether the object be to worship or to fight, to suffer martyrdom or to mete out vengeance, or to effect a solution of social problems too complex to be understood yet too pressing to be postponed.

We note then that the social dislocation appearing at the end of the Time-Scale is occasioned not merely by the fact that the new powers have been appropriated by the few for their own advantage; underlying and conditioning the conflict of material interest between the few and the many is the profound discord between the sophisticated and the unsophisticated levels of apprehension. It is for this reason chiefly that the scientific apprehension available to the exceptional few and applied by them to the mastery of the outer world of things has not been applied to the rational direction of human relations. While the mastery of the physical world has been effected by scientists whose activities, unhampered by the conscious resistance of their subject matter or the ignorance of common men, have been guided by matter-of-fact knowledge and the consciously formulated purpose of subduing things to precisely determined ends, the organization of society has been left to the chance operation of individual self-interest and the uncertain pressure of mass opinion, in the expectation that a beneficence not of man's devising would somehow shape the course of events to a desired but undefined good end.

Not being prophets we cannot foresee either the immediate or the remote outcome of this profound social dislocation. We recall that in the history of mankind it has not infrequently happened that civilizations long established, prosperous, and seemingly secure against mischance have disintegrated, disappeared, and been long forgotten. What has happened before may happen again. Nevertheless, we are not here primarily concerned with the rise and fall of particular civilizations, since we have chosen to observe the progress of mankind in the long-time perspective. In the long-time perspective, from *Pithecanthropus* to Einstein, the progress of mankind, irrespective of the rise and fall of particular civilizations, has been accomplished by the slow, often interrupted, but fairly persistent extension of matter-of-fact knowledge and matter-of-fact apprehension to an ever widening realm of experience. It is only within the last three hundred years that it has been extended to include the entire outer world of Nature and to the forces that are in and behind appearance. Is it then too much to expect that in time to come it will be extended to include the world of human relations?

Whether or not that expectation will in fact be realized we cannot say, but we can guess that what is chiefly required for its realization is time — time and the machines and the harsh pressure of economic distress. The pressure of economic distress will teach men, if anything can, that realities are less dangerous than fancies, that fact-finding is more effective than fault-finding. The machines are already teaching them, and will in the future teach them more effectively perhaps, that a matter-of-fact apprehension of their problems brings the most salutary if not the most inspiring solutions. The machines, not being on the side of the angels, remain impassive in the presence of indignation, wishful thinking, and the moral imperative, but respond without prejudice or comment or ethical reservation to relevant and accurate knowledge impersonally applied. And time, slow-moving, indifferent to men's purposes, in the long-run gives it's validation to matter-of-fact knowledge while dismissing value judgments as useless or insufficiently discriminated.

We at least, having for the moment withdrawn from the market place and the forum in order to take an extended view of human history, can for that purpose afford to give man a little time — three hundred or three thousand years, or ten thousand — to adjust his mental temper and social habits to the dangerous new power that he has as yet only played with but not fully mastered. It seems indeed unlikely that the adjustment can ever be more than clumsily effected so long as the multiplication of implements of power continues to increase the complexity and to accelerate the tempo of social change. But it is conceivable, even probable, that the possibility of discovering and applying new sources and implements of power will in the course of time gradually diminish, or even be altogether exhausted. In that event the outward conditions of life will change less and less rapidly, will in time become sufficiently stable perhaps to be comprehended, sufficiently stable therefore for a relatively complete adjustment of ideas and habits to the relatively unchanging body of matter-of-fact knowledge of man and the outer world in which he lives. In such a stabilized and scientifically adjusted society the idea of progress would no doubt become irrelevant as progress itself became imperceptible or nonexistent.

## 4

We have now taken a hasty glance at human progress, in terms of man's purposes and activities, during the limited period of his observable behavior. For this limited and conditioned view the Olympian Heights were sufficiently remote, the intelligence of the Greek gods was sufficiently extended. But no consideration of human progress can be quite satisfactory that does not view man's purposes and activities under what philosophers call their eternal aspects; and for this view the Olympian Heights will no longer serve, since the universe of time and space has been so greatly expanded beyond anything comprehended by the Greek gods. An eminent mathematician has announced that God is probably a mathematician. Let us assume that he was guilty of a slight error — that he meant to say that a mathematician is probably God. Accompanied by this super-mathematician, we will then make another imaginative flight to some point beyond the finite but unbounded world, and from that point look at man and the universe as they might appear to a cosmic intelligence for whom there are no values except form, extension, and velocity.

Thus conveniently placed, and equipped with cosmic intelligence, we look out upon a universe that comprises perhaps a billion galaxies, each galaxy comprising perhaps ten thousand million stars. If we look long and attentively we may detect, within one of the lesser galaxies, one of the lesser stars which is called the sun; and, circling round this sun, one of its lesser planets which is called the earth. At some moment,

relatively early, in the 150,000 million years which is
the sun's span of life, we note that certain bits of matter on the surface of the earth, by virtue of tempera-
tures not elsewhere obtaining, assume unusually complicated forms and behave in unusually unstable ways.
We understand that certain of these bits of animated
dust distinguish themselves from others, dignify
themselves with the name of Man, and take credit for
having a unique quality which they call intelligence.
They are not aware that intelligence is no merit; the
reverse rather, since it is only an inferior form of energy which Nature has given them in partial compen-
sation for the extreme rapidity with which the law of
entropy $(dS/dt$ is always positive$)$ degrades their vi-
tality. So long as the sun maintains on earth the necessary temperature, these bits of animated matter will
no doubt continue to manifest a perceptible movement, a measurable although diminishing energy. But
their activities, however long continued, are infinitesi-
mal in extent and impotent in effect, of no consequence to the universe, admittedly one of Nature's
indiscretions, worth noting only because rare and unaccountable: of no consequence to the universe, or in
the end to them either, since within a brief moment
of eternal time the light of the sun will inevitably
wane, the earth will grow cold, and all of man's

alleged "imperishable monuments" and "immortal deeds" will be as if they had never been, nor will anything that then is be either better or worse because of anything that man has ever done or ever wished to do.

So a cosmic intelligence might estimate human progress, so it might answer the questions: What is the significance of man? What is the meaning of existence? But then what is this cosmic intelligence that thus asks and answers? It is after all the intelligence of man himself. Apart from man, the cosmos merely is; it does not ask or answer questions. The significance of man is that he is that part of the universe that asks the question, What is the significance of man? He alone can stand apart imaginatively and, regarding himself and the universe in their eternal aspects, pronounce a judgment: The significance of man is that he is insignificant and is aware of it. Man, says Pascal, has this superiority: He knows that the universe can with a breath destroy him, yet at the moment of death he knows that he dies, and knows also the advantage which the universe thereby has over him; but of all that the universe knows nothing.

Of all that, the universe knows nothing. Apart from man, the universe knows nothing at all — nothing of itself or of infinite spaces, nothing of man or of his frustrated aspirations, nothing of beginnings or endings, of progress or retrogression, of life or death, of good or evil fortune. The cosmic view of the universe of infinite spaces, and of man's ultimate fate within it, is man's achievement — the farthest point yet reached in the progressive expansion of human intelligence and power. It is not rightly to be taken as a description of events that are relevant to man's purposes, but rather as an ideal result of those purposes — the manifestation of his insatiable curiosity, his indefeasible determination to know. As such it is less an objective world of fact than man's creation of the world in his own image. It is in truth man's most ingenious invention, his supreme work of art.

A NOTE ON THE TYPE USED IN THIS BOOK

*This book was set on the Linotype in a type-face called "Baskerville." The punches for this face were cut under the supervision of George W. Jones, the eminent English printer and the designer of Granjon and Estienne. Linotype Baskerville is a facsimile cutting from type cast from the original matrices of a face designed by John Baskerville, a writing-master of Birmingham, for his own private press. The original face was the forerunner of the "modern" group of type faces, known today as Scotch, Bodoni, etc. After his death in 1775, Baskerville's punches and matrices were sold in France and were used to produce the sumptuous Kehl edition of Voltaire's works.*

*This book was composed, printed, and bound by The Plimpton Press, Norwood, Massachusetts.*